Impermanence

Embracing change

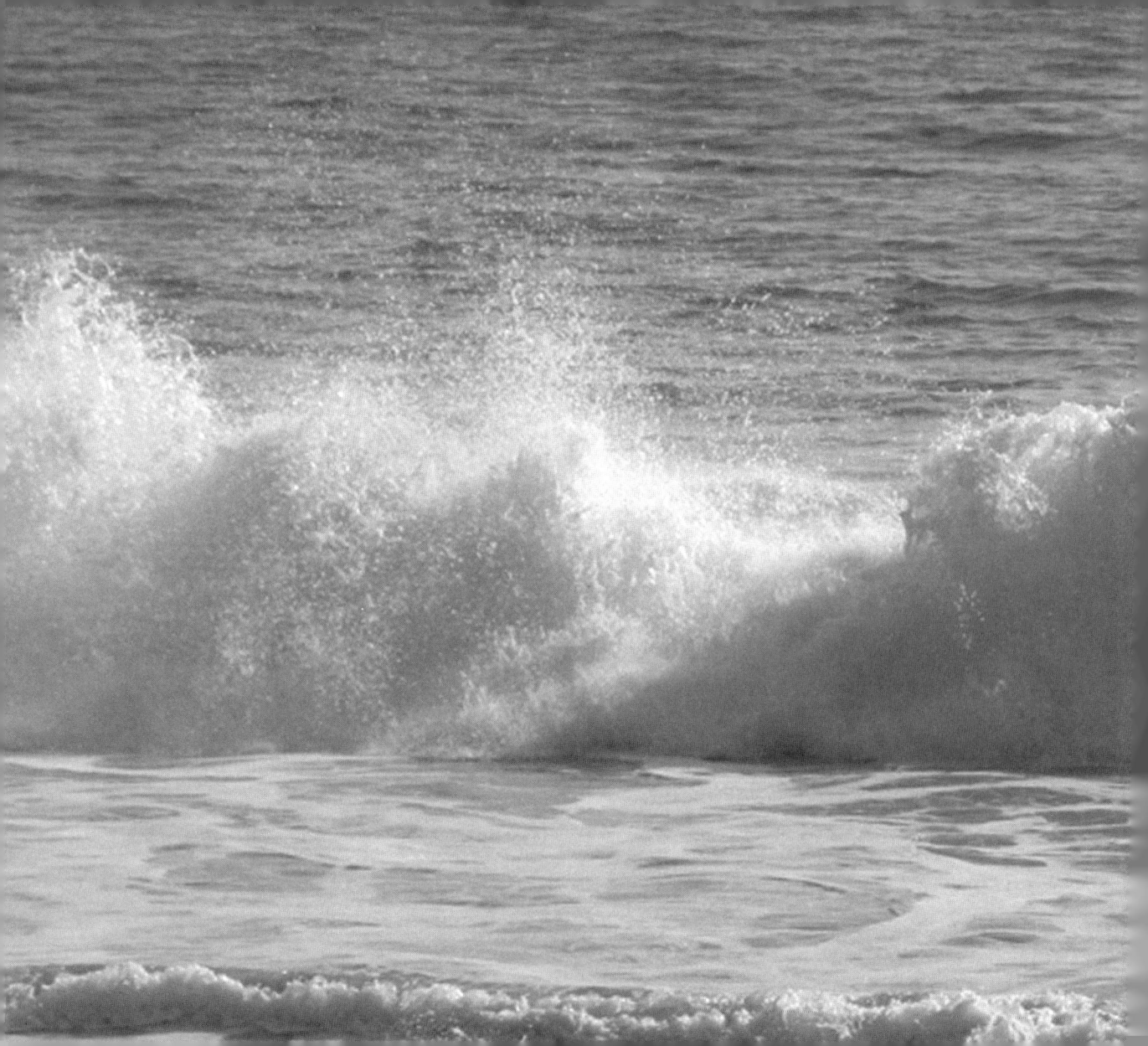

Impermanence

Embracing change

David Hodge & Hi-Jin Kang Hodge

Snow Lion Publications
Ithaca, New York

Snow Lion Publications
P.O. Box 6483
Ithaca, NY 14851 USA
(607) 273-8519
www.snowlionpub.com

Printed in USA.

ISBN 10: 1-55939-307-6
ISBN 13: 978-1-55939-307-2

Library of Congress Cataloging-in-Publication Data

Hodge, David, 1955-
Impermanence: Embracing change / David Hodge & Hi-Jin Kang Hodge;
foreword by H.H. the Dalai Lama.
    p. cm.
ISBN-13: 978-1-55939-307-2 (alk. paper)
ISBN-10: 1-55939-307-6 (alk. paper)
1. Impermanence (Buddhism) 2. Hodge, David, 1955- 3. Hodge, Hi-Jin
Kang, 1974- I. Hodge, Hi-Jin Kang, 1974- II. Title.

BQ4261.H63 2008
294.3'42--dc22   2008023638

For Ann and Young-soo

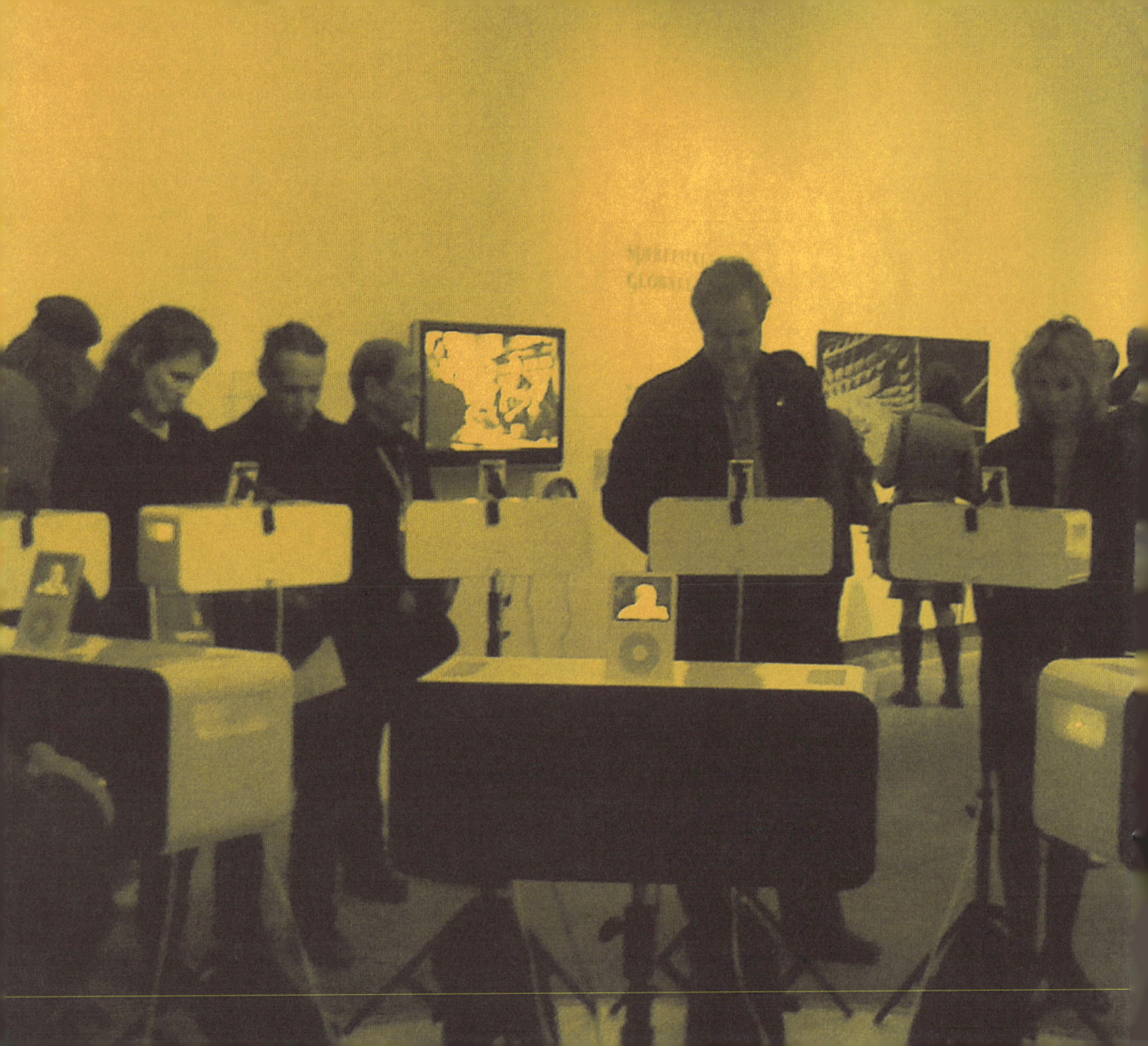

Contents

Impermanence

There is often a big disparity between the way we perceive things and the way things really are. For instance, when we see an object we think, "Oh, this is the very same object which I saw two days ago." This is a very crude way of talking about reality. What is actually happening here is a kind of a conflation between an image or a concept of an entity and the actual reality of the moment. In reality, the object or entity that we are perceiving has already gone through a lot of stages. It is dynamic, it is transient, it is momentary, so the object that we are perceiving now is not the same as the one we perceived a day ago or two days ago, but we have the impression that we are perceiving the very same thing because what we are doing is conflating our concept of that object and the actual object. By grasping for permanence, we cause things to appear to us differently than how they actually exist.

It is vital to leave a lot of room for change in one's relations to another person. Change comes about in times of transition, allowing love actually to ripen and expand. Then one is able to really know the other one – to see that person with their faults and weaknesses and going through change, a human being like oneself. Only at this stage can there be true love.

The Dalai Lama

An exhibition of works by contemporary artists celebrating the life and works of the Dalai Lama, co-sponsored by the Dalai Lama Foundation and the Committee of 100 for Tibet, is currently touring major museums and galleries in the U.S. and throughout the world. This show, titled "The Missing Peace," interweaves the perspectives of 89 artists and artist collaboratives from twenty-five different countries around themes and ideals associated with the Dalai Lama, such as exile, compassion, peace, and change.

One of the exhibition's most powerful and thought-provoking pieces is an installation titled "Impermanence" by multi-media artists David Hodge and Hi-Jin Kang Hodge. It explores the central Buddhist concept of impermanence and how this concept affects people in a variety of ways. The Hodges interviewed over a hundred people from diverse walks of life. Their installation consists of a large, circular arrangement of mounted iPods on which the interviews play on their own screens, both simultaneously and sequentially, mimicking the ebb and flow of conversation in a room full of people.

The results of the Hodges' work are more varied than anyone could have expected, and very intimate. Some of the interview subjects saw impermanence as a source of dread, while some saw it as providing occasions for a greater appreciation of life. Many people spoke about very personal things that deeply impacted their life and outlook. But the strong theme that emerges from reading these accounts and watching the DVD is not one of depression or hopelessness over the unavoidable changes we all experience. Rather, there is a powerful theme of awakening—the sense that chaos and change offer the opportunity to develop greater flexibility in negotiating life situations and that, no matter what, there will always be new possibilities available in the world and in our lives.

~

Overview

Impermanence is an idea which Tibetans use as an effective tool to find a balance between the highs and lows we experience in life. While we know that the idea of impermanence has more subtle explanations in Buddhism, it is generally understood in a simple, natural way as meaning that all things are constantly subject to change; the physical world is disintegrating moment by moment, and our mental state is in constant flux.

By accepting the fact that nothing we feel and see remains constant, we remind ourselves of the futility of clinging to strong emotions towards that which we possess physically, such as treasured objects, or even to our feelings of love, anger, hurt, and other conflicted emotions towards friend, family, or foe.

Whenever there are disappointments—an unfulfilled wish, a broken promise, an expectation gone wrong—impermanence reminds us that while they cannot be undone, they are not permanent, and that their intensity diminishes with the passage of time.

Just as the lesson of impermanence helps us to deal with our disappointments, it also helps us to temper the highs of successes we achieve or the euphoria of dreams fulfilled. Impermanence reminds us that they too do not last indefinitely, and that we should not be carried away by our great joys because if we are, there will be no cushion to land on when we come down.

Simply taught, impermanence reminds us that everything we experience is subject to change, both positive and negative, and that this realization can temper our emotions and help us find greater stability and peace within ourselves.

Tenzin N. Tethong
President, The Dalai Lama Foundation

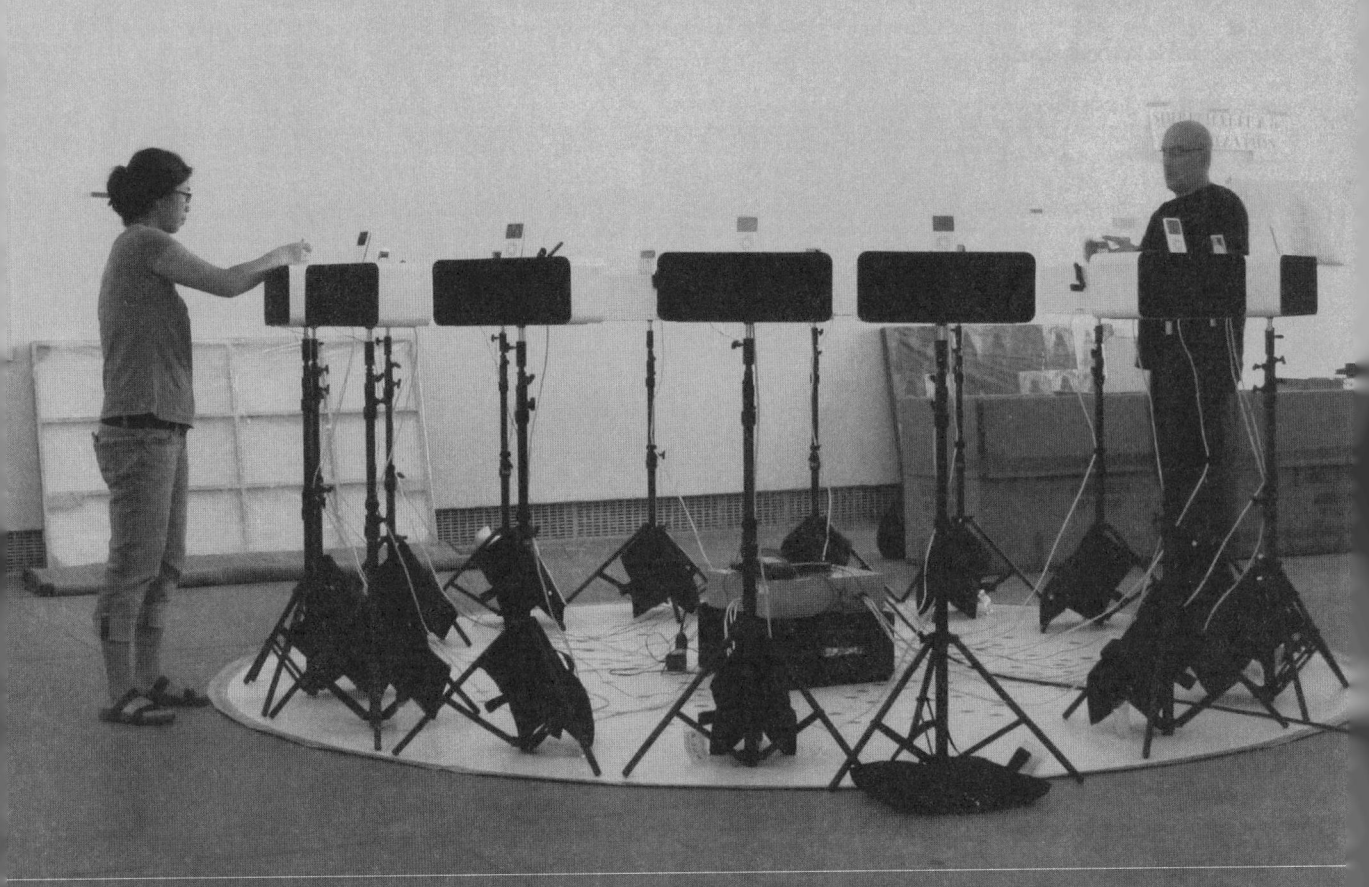

The Artists' Perspective

This project began as an installation for an exhibition called *The Missing Peace: Artists Consider the Dalai Lama*. The exhibition had called on artists to pick one of a number of Buddhist themes, and we chose impermanence.

The reasons for our choice were many, but we were probably most affected by an experience we had recently had while filming for a project about a cancer survivor. She was a bright, vibrant woman who had confronted her disease with great courage and humanity. When we started, she had seemingly won her fight and was eager to share her experience with others. We spent a month filming her, her friends, and her husband about what they had learned from her struggle. Then, about halfway through our work, her cancer virulently returned and took her from us.

This experience led us to wonder if others had similar stories about impermanence in its most extreme form: death. We set out with a vague plan. We'd turn on our cameras and ask people to talk about the topic.

It took only one interview to learn that we had struck a chord. While few people talk openly with one another about impermanence, we learned that many had thought deeply about the subject. In subsequent interviews, we were surprised by how wise people could be when they finally decided to address this subject.

It wasn't merely the religious and spiritual thinkers who proved the most interesting. One of our best interviews was with a man who had come by our house to wash our windows. He was from Jamaica, and because we had a little difficulty with each other's accents, he didn't immediately understand what we meant by "impermanence." While we were explaining it, he suddenly said, "Oh, you mean, you are on fire." We thought, what a great way to talk about impermanence.

In the end, it was responses like his that helped make our installation what it was. We presented all of the interviews, edited by topic, in a circle of video iPods. Sometimes their voices spoke collectively; at other times, a single voice could be heard above the rest. The effect allowed viewers to listen in, just as we had, to 122 people talking about impermanence.

This book and DVD are the latest evolution of the project. They present the ideas of those we interviewed, together with topical essays by a number of prominent thinkers. We are not trying to draw any conclusions. Instead, the words and images you find here should allow you to listen and perhaps take part in a discussion about impermanence. Like our subjects you may find that while you rarely speak openly about this topic, you have thought about it very much indeed.

David Hodge and Hi-Jin Kang Hodge

IMPERMANENCE

I tend to embrace impermanence as a recognition of a reality of aliveness.

Spiritual Evolution in a World of Change
B. Alan Wallace

Change—it's one of the few constants in life. All that we can really count on is that everything we experience inside and outside ourselves will change—in fact, it's always changing with every passing moment. What we can't count on is how things will change, whether to our benefit or harm. A second constant in our lives is our perpetual wish for freedom from fear and suffering, and our yearning for security and happiness. Those two constants present us with one of the most fundamental challenges of our existence: In light of the ever-changing nature of our bodies, minds, and the world around us, how can we possibly achieve any lasting sense of well-being? Given how little we can control in terms of the natural environment, others' behavior, and even our own bodies and minds, is it hopeless to think we might ever find a safe haven, protected from the storms of change?

Buddhism calls the world of our experience the "desire realm," for in our pursuit of happiness, we constantly look outward to objects—including people, places, activities, and situations—that we view as desirable. If only we could acquire or be involved with these objects of our desire, we believe, we could find the peace and joy that is our heart's desire. We may identify desirable objects in even closer proximity: in states of our own bodies and minds, hoping that they will provide us with the satisfaction we seek. But all these appearances are constantly in a state of flux, changing from moment to moment in unpredictable and uncontrollable ways, and it's only a matter of time before they pass from view altogether. The more deeply we probe the reality of impermanence, the more it becomes apparent that none of these sensory objects is a true source of happiness. By failing to recognize this simple truth, we cling to appearances as being more durable than they are, and we then devote our lives to the futile pursuit to secure pleasant, desirable objects, people, and situations. Like an organism that perishes due to its failure to adapt to a changing environment, we hurtle ourselves against the relentless reality of impermanence until we perish from sheer exhaustion. The appearances to our senses are not the source of our frustration, misery, and despair. Rather, it is our clinging and attachment to them that causes us ceaseless unrest and dissatisfaction.

Once we have discovered that the true source of our unhappiness does not lie outside ourselves, we may seek out the causes of our anxiety and discontent in terms of our own behavior, assumptions, thoughts, emotions, and attitudes. How does our way of engaging with the world contribute to our own and others' discontent? By examining the repercussions of our own mental states and conduct, we may identify specific ways that we harm ourselves and others out of ignorance. And once we have identified these true causes of suffering, we can gradually weed them out and see for ourselves whether we experience less distress in our daily lives. This is the first step in spiritual evolution, as we learn to adapt our behavior in ways that support our own and others' well-being.

On this basis, we can take the further step in spiritual evolution of applying effective means—specifically by way of meditation—to calm the inner turbulence of the mind. As the obsessive and compulsive tendencies of the mind subside, we may become increasingly aware of the ground state of the mind when it is unperturbed by agitation and distraction. Buddhist contemplatives who have explored the inner recesses of the mind have discovered that the "natural state" of the mind is one of bliss, luminosity, and stillness. These qualities are unveiled when the mind settles in a state of clarity and inner calm. The bliss that emerges from such equilibrium is not contingent upon pleasurable stimuli or desirable objects—not even happy thoughts or positive attitudes—rather, it is a quality of well-being that arises when the mind is free of disruptive desires, thoughts, and emotions. Like an underground current of pure spring water, this continuum of awareness arises from moment to moment, untouched by the vicissitudes of the world around us. By withdrawing the physical senses into the domain of the mind and by settling the mind in its natural state, we discover an inner haven of peace. But as soon as we emerge from this tranquil state of meditative withdrawal, we are thrown back into the ever-changing world of appearances.

If the root of suffering is ignorance and confusion, as Buddhism maintains, then the root of happiness must lie in understanding and wisdom, and not simply in retracting our awareness from the world around us. This is where the practice of insight meditation comes in: with discerning mindfulness we attend closely to the reality of the present moment without attachment or aversion, without confusing our conceptual projections with the perceptual realities that rise up to meet us from moment to moment. Through the close examination of our bodies, our minds, and our relation to other living beings and the environment at large, we may align our view of reality with the way things really are. This is the greatest step in spiritual evolution, and it results in an enduring sense of well-being that arises from knowing reality as it is. As if waking up within a dream, we discover our own freedom that brings with it a truth-given joy.

Awareness of impermanence can provide us with the inspiration to probe our own nature, to tap into the deepest dimensions of our own awareness, and to overcome the kinds of confusion that lie at the root of suffering and discontent. The Buddha declared that just as the elephant makes the deepest of footprints, so does the awareness of impermanence make the deepest impact in terms of transforming our aspirations, getting to the root of suffering, and opening the way to liberation and enlightenment.

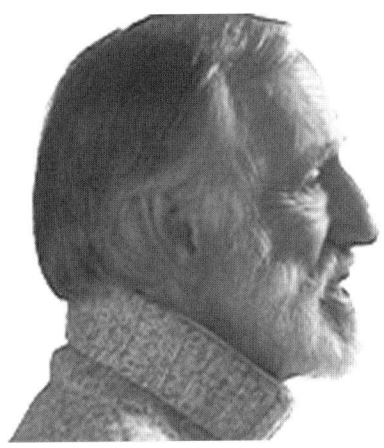

Impermanence, I see it as being foundational.
How can you have creation, if there's not impermanence?
So every aspect of aliveness seems to carry with it a temporary nature. The more I reflected on it, the less I began to think of it in terms of a completion or a finishing or an ending but as being foundation to a beginning.
Being at the essence of life as I experience life, I tend to embrace impermanence as a recognition of a reality of aliveness.

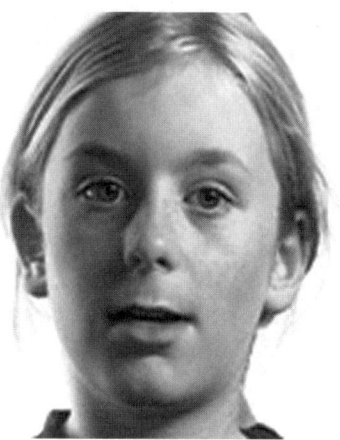

Impermanence means change. Change just happens. Over time everything changes. Without change I think I wouldn't be doing very well. I don't think anything would have happened without change, and change just happens.

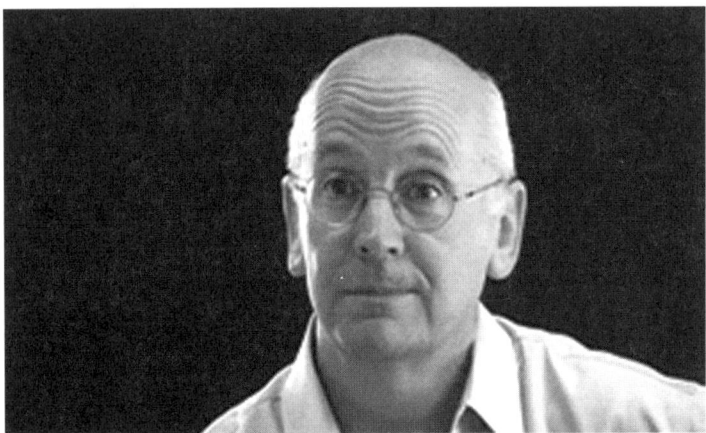

It's the condition of letting go and being in the habit of letting go. Being detached. It's the stage of being able to enjoy what is in its passing away without trying to cling to it.

A beggar on the side of the road, he has nothing, he puts out his hand saying "give me a dime" and the hand is open, open to what may be given by life. And somebody passing by drops a quarter in his hand, and immediately the hand closes to possess it and it becomes a fist. Then you can use the fist to protect what you have possessed. But of course you can't even use it very well because you are so intent on clinging to it and protecting it.

Poverty of spirit is now opening the hand again, having the courage and taking the risk of remaining open. Running the risk the quarter may be taken away from you but also being in a position where you can receive more.

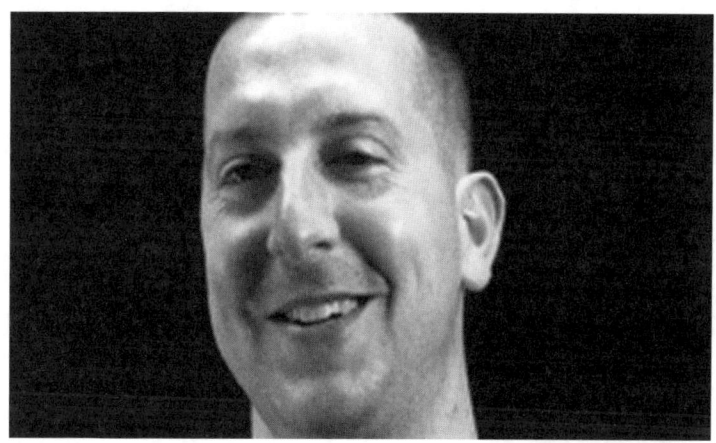

My initial reaction is a negative one like "oh, change is not good..." But then I had to stop and realize there are a lot of changes that happen that are positive. Some kind of violent encounter and seeing the lives that are changed when someone dies—in that case if change does not happen it's a bad thing.

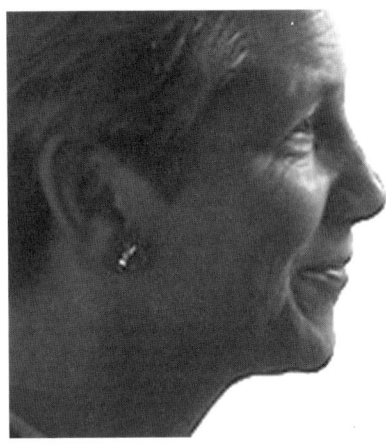

Everything is always changing, people are changing, environments are changing. It's interesting to watch everything moving and if you look at the ocean, that's a perfect example of impermanence. Ebbing and flowing, that's constant life force, changing all the time.

If you try to stop or make everything stop around you and not change, that's when I think unhappiness is created. It festers.

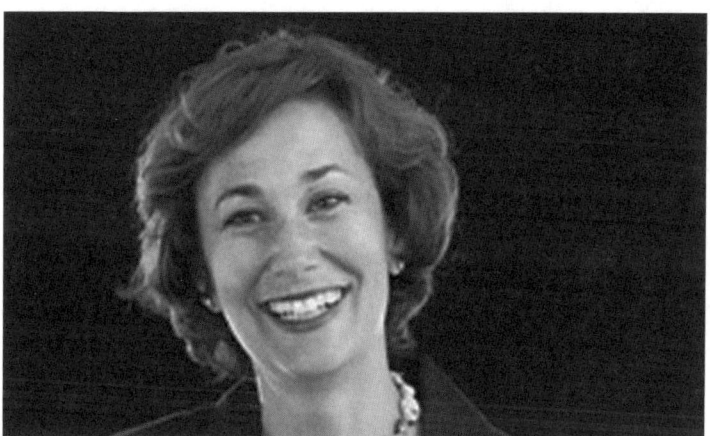

We are all just passing through. Nothing bad lasts forever. Flip side to that is if something is really great, you also know that that's not going to last so you really have to enjoy the moment you are in and appreciate it for what it is.

It's a good thing that we are all just passing through because I think that every single person can have tremendous impact in the way that they touch other people while they are here and that's what's ultimately important.

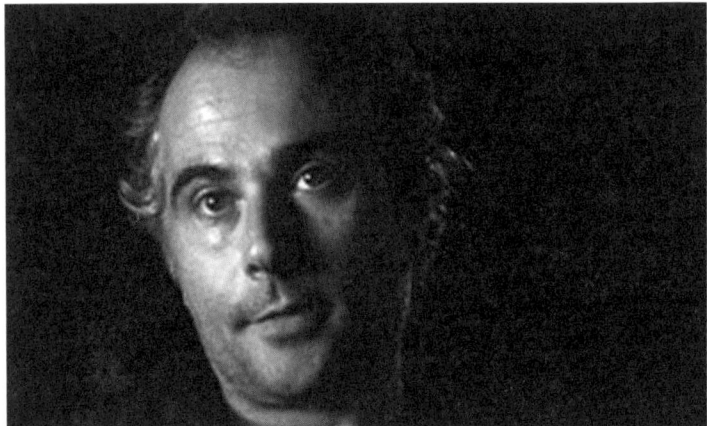

If we observe nature, we come to the conclusion that all things are impermanent. Things are always coming out of nothingness and going into nothingness. Me and you are just temporary vehicles. We are impermanent,
here to stay for a while.

Impermanence for me is the act of waking up every morning and knowing I am waking up every morning.

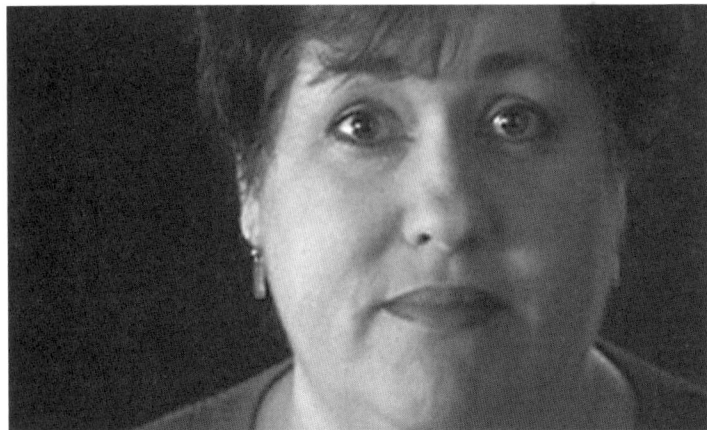

Impermanence is living without denial.

It's really easy to deny that we aren't here forever. It is easier to just not think about how fragile life is.

This moment will not occur again. It can all be taken away.

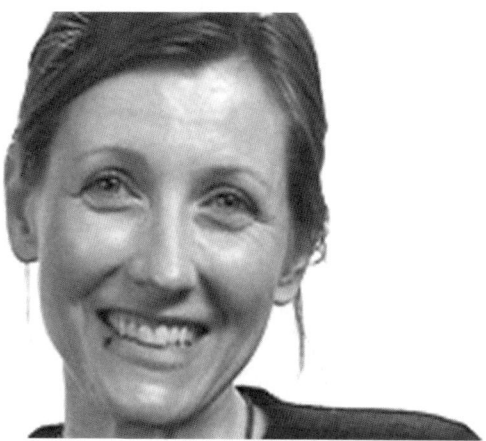

When you can't control something it brings up a lot of fear and part of that is everything is changing constantly. I think that's one of the best things about impermanence. It can really lend an air of excitement to life. Any minute, something different can happen if you are open to it.

Now that I accept impermanence, I find life so much more exciting. Sometimes impermanence can be really good and sometimes it really sucks but it's the only thing you can rely on.

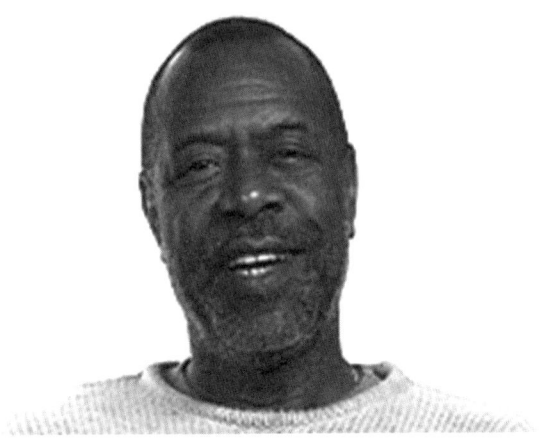

My life started out in impermanence. When I was ten, my mother passed. That was one of the real realities for me of an impermanence. Because I always felt up to that point, she will always be there.

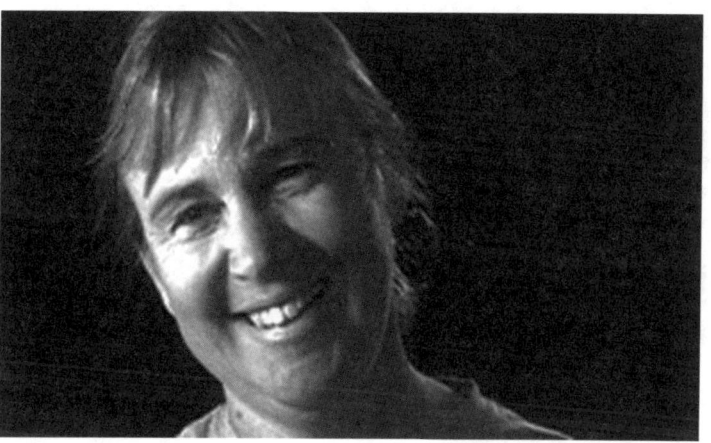

I suppose you could say impermanence is what drives life since if everything stayed the same, nothing would change and we would be stuck in a pattern. I can't even imagine how people would live if nothing changed. If you woke up and everything was the same, that would be like a machine. Maybe that's where we are headed.

What would one do if one wasn't dealing with change? You could probably figure everything out in one day and you would not have anything to do for the rest of your life. That would be kind of a short road. We can't really direct change. It changes and it never goes back to what it was but it's always moving out towards future things.

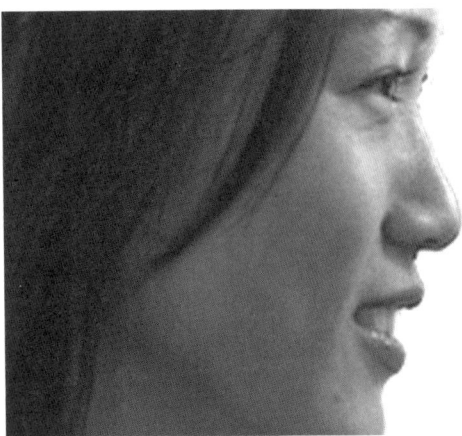

It's a connection. Maybe in some ways we are all interconnected. If you realize you are connected somehow to a bigger plan, then it takes away a lot of fear and it gives you a lot of hope and confidence.

Uncertainty is actually positive. You start to realize that a lot of uncertainty is emotional response. It's not meant to be feared. Maybe highlight the fact that there are some things we can control and some things we cannot. The essence of impermanence is that you are not trying to struggle against what you really want, but trying to let go and allow things to naturally come to be. You are here to live out a great life and enjoy what life has to offer but at the same time be very respectful of the opportunity you are given and try not to be insisting on "I want things in my way." You have to let go.

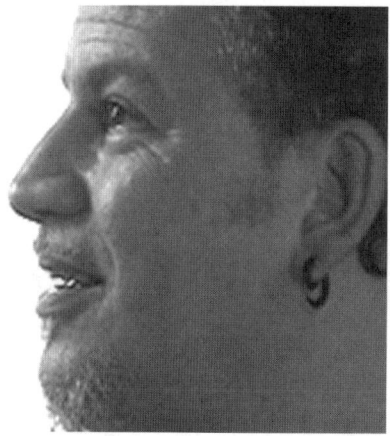

When I think of the word impermanence, I think the first thing that happens is most parts of me get scared. I feel like this is not where I am from. There's nothing just and there are no guarantees, there's lots of chaos.

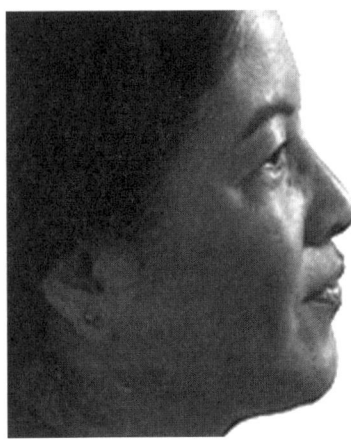

I see impermanence as a big river we are all swimming in. How all things are always changing and evolving and disappearing and reemerging into different forms.

Impermanence impacts my daily life in the sense that my awareness of it is not to hold things too tightly.

Everything around me is part of something that does not belong to me in a sense because I don't really belong to myself in another sense. When I die, none of this is going to matter at all and the only thing that's going to matter is what I have done and what I have left behind.

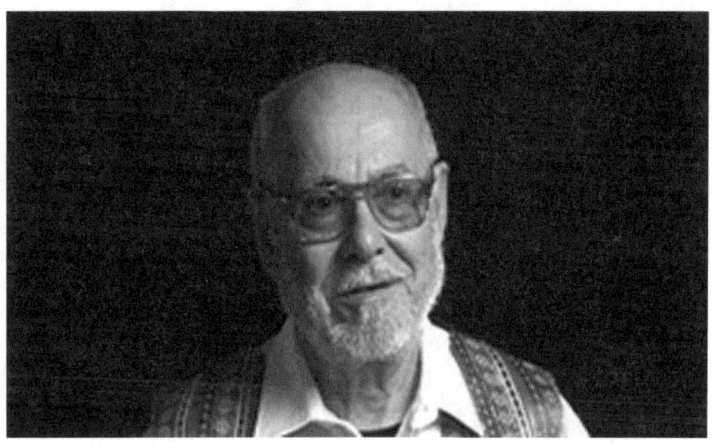

Reality, a bowl of mercury.
You think you can hold it, yet it slips from and between your fingers.

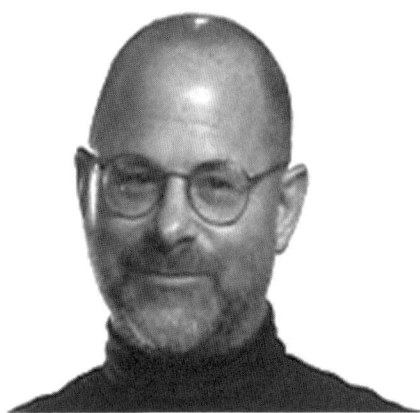

Almost everything in life is a little bit like skiing. It doesn't really work if you are standing still. It only works if you are moving. One of the things about moving and skiing is that you never are really in control. I'm never in control. You have to be okay with being a little bit out of control and find a balance that you can keep up as long as you can and still be out of control enough so you keep going down the hill.

Being aware that change is going to happen whether I like it or not. I can choose to go with it or I can try to not go with it but it's going to take me anyway.

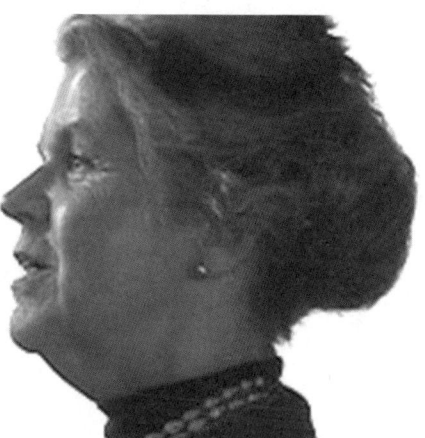

When I think of impermanence, I think of the things that fall away through time. For me, impermanence is connected with time while permanence is anything that transcends time or that continues through time into the timeless.

I had an experience being homeless. It was like being a fish in water. You are not aware of the water until you leave the water. Everything felt very transitory, very impermanent, very temporary.

AWARENESS

My body was betraying me. It was taking over and doing things I couldn't control.

The Mind That Wakes Up
Kay Larson

Let's pause for a moment to consider how things really are. Everything is impermanent, and the sting of that realization bites into the skin like a whip drawing blood from an exhausted racehorse. But is pain and suffering the whole story? Perhaps there is something else to see. The Buddha posed that challenge to a woman in his world, and the lesson still applies.

Kisa Gotami has led a sheltered life, according to the *Dhammapada*. Married to the son of a rich merchant, she feels immune from death. But then her son dies before he can walk. Deep in shock and denial, she refuses to let the body be burnt. Slinging the tiny corpse on her hip, she rages through the neighborhood, asking if anyone knows where she might find medicine to bring him back to life. Most people think she's crazy, but a wise man recognizes a spiritual crisis when he sees it, and sends her to the Buddha.

The Buddha tells her he knows where to find the medicine she needs. To create it, he will require a pinch of white mustard seed from a household where no one has ever died. Kisa Gotami begins knocking on doors. The *Dhammapada* observes: "At every house she is told, 'The living are few, but the dead are many.'" We can imagine the heads shaking back and forth. Realization slowly penetrates her grief, and light dawns. Without so much as a single mustard seed in hand, she returns to the Buddha and tells him that she now knows that every living thing must die. Although the *Dhammapada* doesn't say it, we recognize the horizon that she now glimpses—the ring of light circling her suffering. Through the power of this teaching, she becomes a nun. One day she notices that the flickering of a lamp is like the life of all of us. She takes the leap of liberation and becomes an arhat—one who has "laid down the burden."

What did the Buddha offer her? Only awareness. Yet what a tool.

How are things, really? They change. What if nothing changed? Stop to contemplate that thought. Visualize everything suddenly freezing. Kurt Vonnegut did exactly that in *Cat's Cradle*, which contains a tale about ice-nine, a new crystal that would cause water to turn to ice at 114.4 degrees. When ice-nine fell into water, the world went into lock-down. Vonnegut reportedly based his idea on a suggestion made by a Nobel Prize winning chemist, Irving Langmuir, to H. G. Wells during a tour of General Electric in the 1930s. Even if a joke, the thought is alarming.

In a sense, it doesn't matter how awareness arises: whether it's accompanied by grief, rage, anxiety, wailing, or radical acceptance (the less painful way). Awareness is everything. It's everything because it reconnects us to fundamental truths that are bigger than we are. In his long night of realization under the bodhi tree, the Buddha reached the highest levels of awareness, up there where the morning star shines diamond-like in a pre-dawn sky, way up where everyone below can see it, just by looking up, at any point from horizon to horizon. The aspect he saw is now called Buddha-mind. Everything is empty, in truth: empty of all the ego constructs that burden us. Empty of frozenness and changelessness; empty of illusions. Empty of being and yet suffused with being. Stones, trees, water, monkeys, us—there is an aspect of our nature that is unborn and undying, limitless and luminous. All of creation shines in the light of this aspect. To become aware of it is to lay down many burdens.

If we focus entirely on our suffering, we circle around and around our own ego-constructs, like oxen yoked to an old mill wheel. The oxen may glimpse the green fields filled with lovely grasses, but the possibility of grazing there is just a dream. Knowing this, the Buddha reminded us that there is an Eightfold Path. It's a series of steps to clarify what's true, and to practice the truth in one's life.

The Buddhist sutras are filled with observations that access this highest awareness. The Heart Sutra says: form (the created world) is empty (not bounded, not limited; a projection of what the Tibetans call "pure light mind"). The Flower Garland Sutra says that once ego gets out of the way, the walls that separate us lose all semblance of reality. We realize that we live in a vast web of interconnection and interpenetration linking all beings. Each one of us—each thing throughout space and time—is the Buddha, and is not independent of all other Buddhas. The Lotus Sutra says that hearing this teaching will immediately liberate you.

Animals are stuck in their suffering because they lack awareness; yet they are also able to live in the moment because they are not trapped in discursive thoughts. Kisa Gotami was suffering because she was trapped in a discursive thought: an idea that nothing should die. Yet, being human, she could rise to a level of awareness that saw her thought as a kind of enslavement: ego ordering the universe to obey what ego wants. Liberation from that all-too-human viewpoint is the beginning of the Eightfold Path, and of practicing as a Buddhist. It's also broader. It's the beginning of recognizing the frame of our existence and the heart that each of us was born with. To practice awareness in its fullest sense is to join one's light with the diamond-bright morning star. Then everything is already liberated. One need only see it.

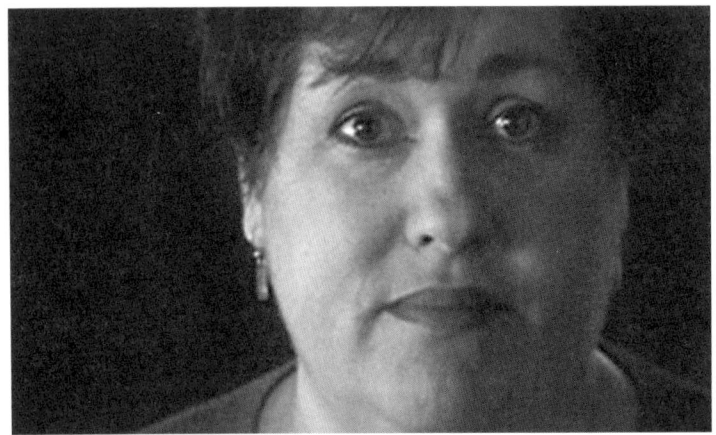

My lesson in impermanence has come in the form of cancer. The joy of impermanence is that it allows to me to appreciate, and value and cherish because it can all be gone. I get that now.

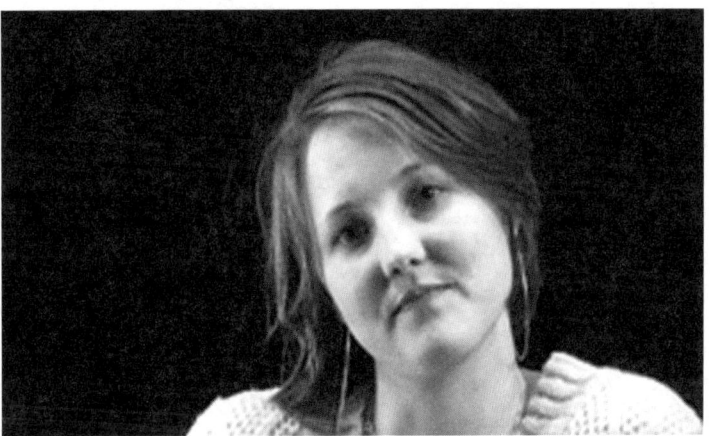

Probably the first time my heart broke. First relationship ending.
It wasn't so much that I thought it would last forever but that you don't have
to think about an ending until it ends.

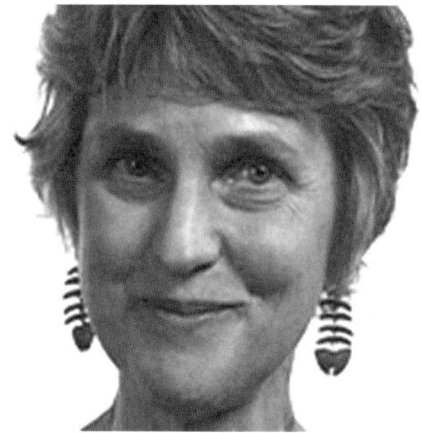

When I was thirteen, I started growing boobs and I realized I was changing. That was kind of an awkward moment. My body was betraying me. I
really liked the way I was when I was seven and a little bit freer to do what
I wanted. But all of a sudden, my body was taking over and doing things I
couldn't control. And it kept doing it and in fact it is still doing it.
In some way, that seven-year-old is still inside my psyche and my soul. But
the only place I can show you that seven-year-old is in my family album. You
can't really document the inner self of a person. You can't really photograph
me at almost sixty as a seven-year-old and yet, I'm still that seven-year-old
somewhere inside myself.

PERMANENCE

One permanent thing is impermanence.

Men and Women

Men and women in white cotton gloves walk hushed, reverent
down hallways, in and out of temperature controlled rooms,
holding archival boxes like wafers at the altar.

Art is their job—choosing it, preserving it, presenting it
within structures of marbled magnificence—towering structures
built to last, but they don't because

other men and women working with their gloves off
have another job—and their job is War. These men and women
working down on the ground or up in the air, carry out the dirtier work

of other men and women suited in civility,
camouflaged in cleanliness—whose job it is
to sanction chaos, target countries like carnival prizes—countries that

still other men and women call home.

Meanwhile, men and women in white cotton gloves
continue down the hallways toward imagined eternity
carrying and protecting the work of the masters who are

other men and women lucky enough to have
jobs of creation like a mother or God.
But in fact, they're just like all the rest—

graced as they are with the extraordinary opportunity of now.

Only their calling requires them to be open to the mystery,
to let it move through them into matter which might last
—no longer really than they themselves.

© Lucy Hilmer 2008
March 15- April 2, 2008

The Archivist's Truth

I keep what I can and store it away
for the day when there's time to
sort through what I've saved
from the mountains I've climbed
and creek beds I've wandered.

Some day when there's time
I'll revisit my collection—these pieces of
rock face chipped off in a storm, these once wet pebbles
picked up by my own hands to remember how it felt
being me in the glow of my going.

My hands from their tiniest, tenderest state
to their calloused and age-spotted now
have always contained clues to their own mystery.
I can open them like a book and it's all there to be read
—the truth of their circling sojourn to stillness.

But my hands have always tried so hard to hold on
to what can't be kept, and they should know better.
They should know that what counts can never be
saved in cardboard boxes, and that what lives
can never be described, and especially by stone.

© Lucy Hilmer 2008
March 26-April 2, 2008

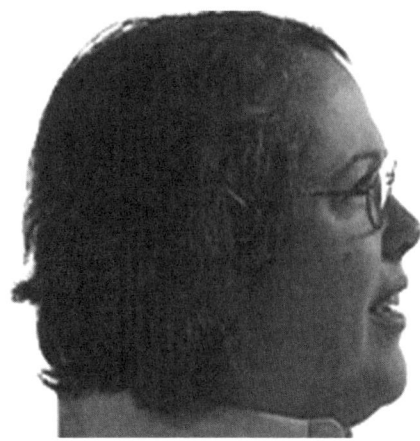

It's almost like you have to have permanence to enjoy the impermanence. If you weren't the physical body here at this point and time which is a very permanent kind of thing in that moment, you wouldn't be able to appreciate the complete impermanence of the world.

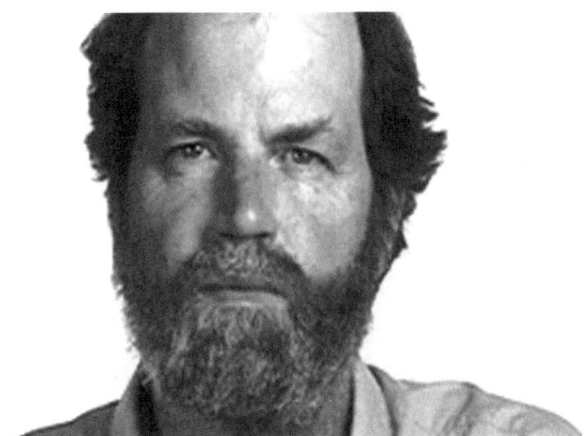

Only thing that is really permanent is probably change.
Society is having a hard time keeping up with change.
Just because you have technology doesn't mean that you have the psychology to deal with it.

Our construct for reality is based on trying to say things are fixed, but on the other hand, they are really not.

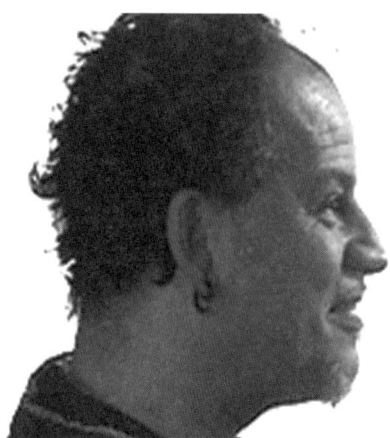

As much as I need a permanent idea for getting up every morning and accomplishing something for feeling good, then I need the other idea of impermanence to keep myself sane and not so goal-oriented. So I feel like it's a balancing act and if I can get in the middle of it, that's when I'm happy.

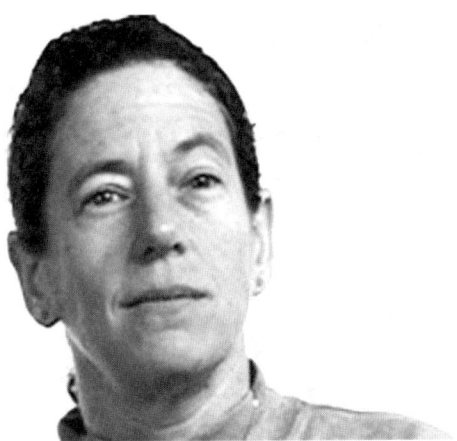

I see impermanence and permanence as a happy balance.
There has to be impermanence with permanence in equal amounts. It's kind
of like we are helium balloons but we need to be held.

I don't think I ever realized what permanence was until I met my partner.
There's such a total connection there and it has been there from day one.
The goal for anybody is to head back to that oneness with another person.
Even though our bodies go away, it's just about our oneness of our energy.

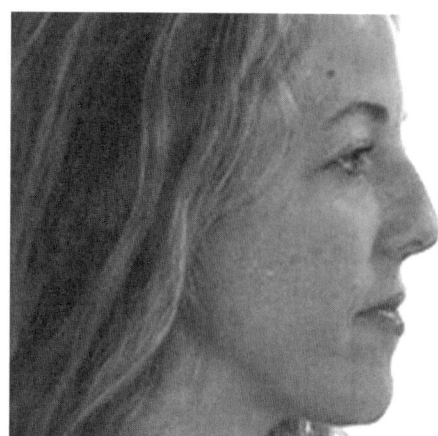

We need to act as if things and people and ideas are permanent or they are true or valuable.

You couldn't marry someone unless he was there to stay. You wouldn't love people if you are always thinking about how they would die or stop loving you. You have to imagine a person as somehow joined to and part of and constituted by the world they live in.

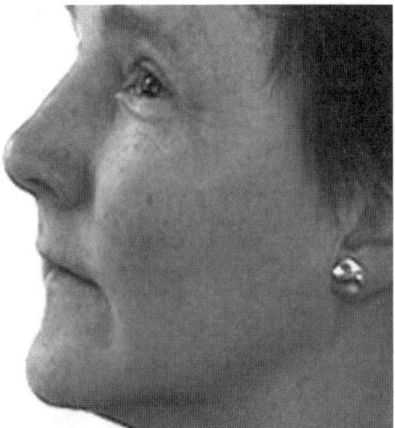

We are sort of hard-wired in a way to think and to believe in permanence, that things are always going to be the same. Even children in normal development, they need some sense of permanence in their life to develop normally. It comes down to some basic needs of security. I don't think we give that up necessarily when we are adults. Because people don't like to experience it, people don't like to feel that things are going to change.

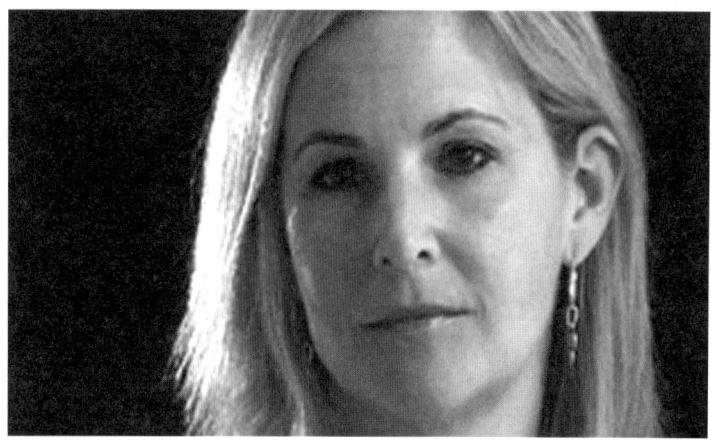

I love the people I love.
I love them every day, I love them in any way. That's permanent.

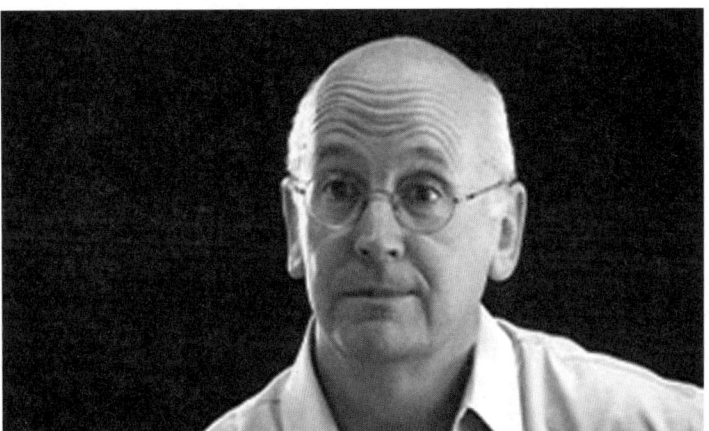

Anything you could point to and say that's permanent will probably dissolve on you. But things that you can't point to or define or objectify, I think there is continuity and permanence. There is something beyond permanence and impermanence and that is presence. The closest we come to really experiencing that personally in the fullness of experience is love.

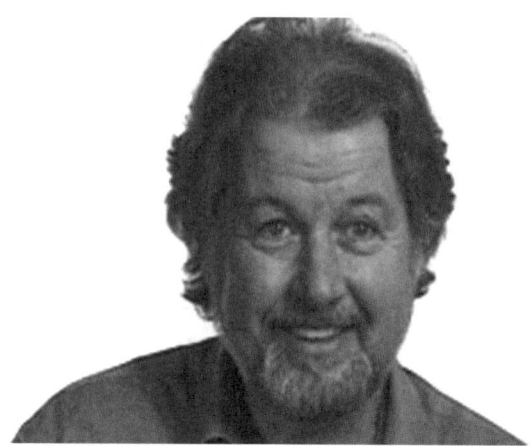

You're a spirit being that came here to learn and to grow. And the spirit doesn't die when you die. Spirit lives on in some form. So that's not impermanent, that essence part of me, that's not something that I feel is fleeting.

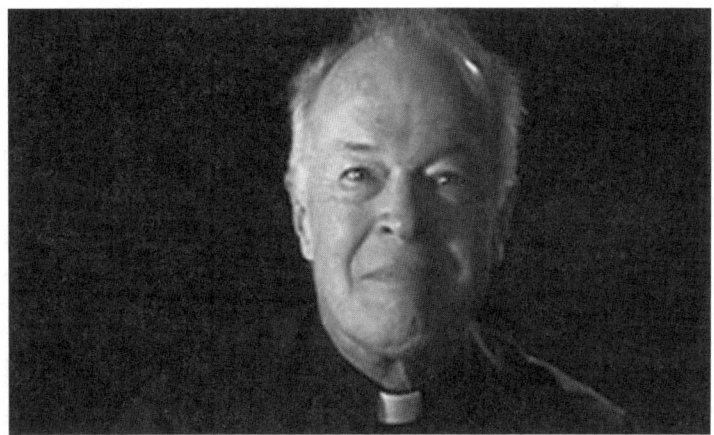

Faith, hope and love.
We are just passing through this life. We are born to live, to die, to live forever.

We are not human beings trying to live spiritually, we are spiritual beings trying to live humanly. That's the challenge, to be human. We are spirit of our very nature.

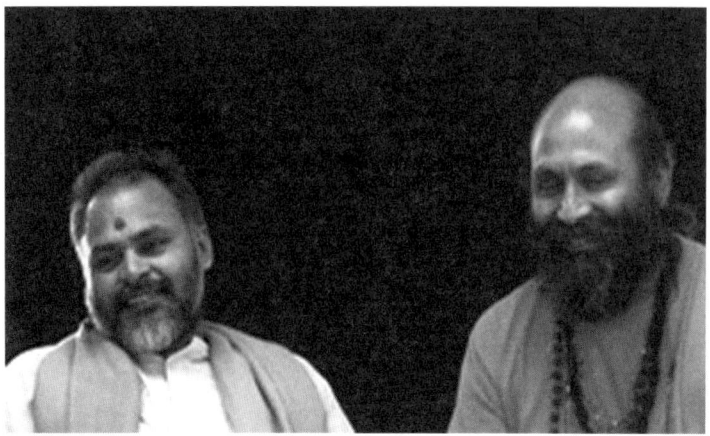

What is permanent in life is the peace that comes from your soul, in other words knowing who you are, brings you the peace.

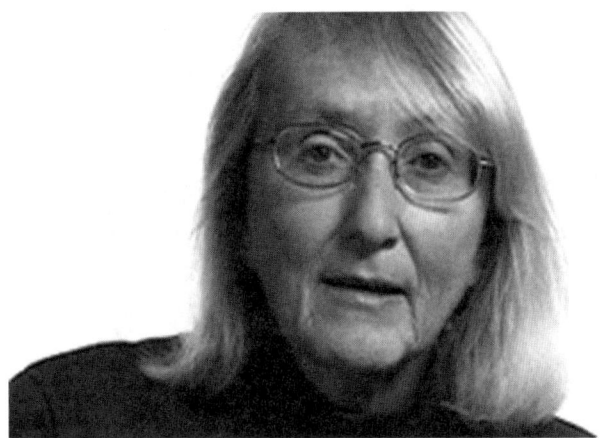

There's something about the life force that wants to keep going. Part of it is consciousness, part of it is loving that state of consciousness. The larger part of it is that joy and vitality that people experience as being alive.

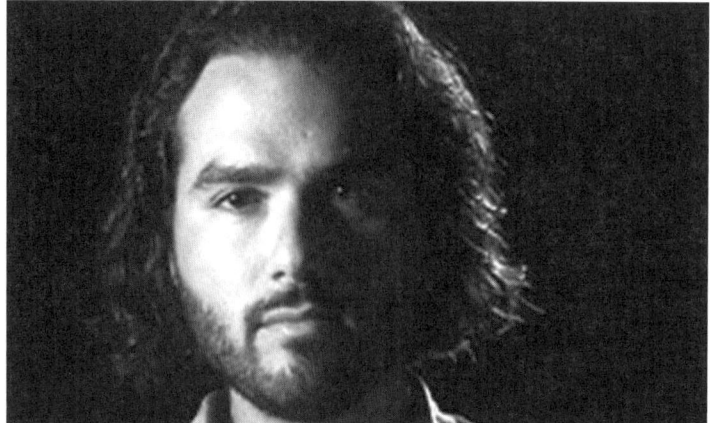

In a lot of ways things that are permanent help make things more efficient. So if we can establish a few fixed points, what we call fix points, we can build fluid systems around them. Choosing things that appear permanent to us on our level of existence can be practically helpful. Just like speed limits and legal legislations. They just help us.

The habit is to see something as being permanent and another thing as impermanent, perhaps reaching out for permanence as a way of comfort or of reassurance.

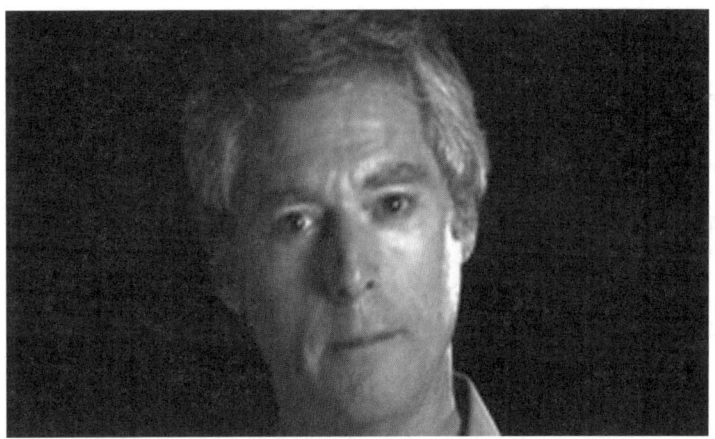

As the Buddhist tradition says as a whole, impermanence is always there. We have no vacations from the reality of impermanence. There are some things we can count on and that is one of them.

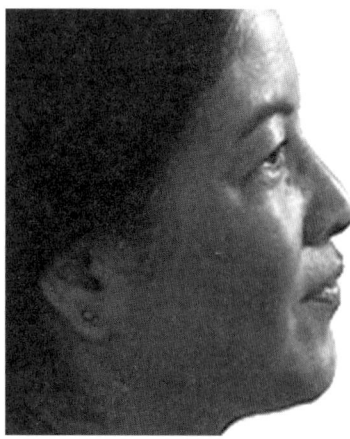

Death is certain. It's the time that is uncertain. And it could be today or tomorrow, next year or thirty years. You don't know. Death really is constant.

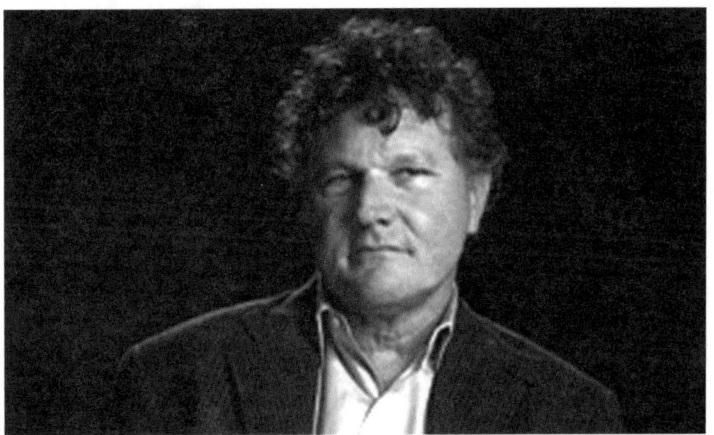

Permanence is an abstraction. Permanence is the thing which there's no evidence of anywhere. It can take a lifetime, and it's rare that you get a satisfying formulation and yet, you keep encountering the idea.

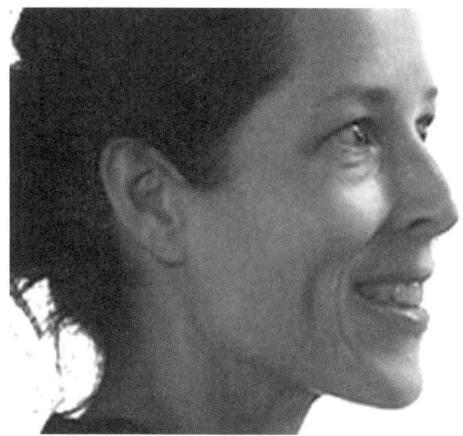

Permanence is really hard. The things we do to manipulate a sense of permanence. I don't think about leaving anything behind. I don't want to leave anything behind. It seems really burdensome when people create something that is even permanent for your lifetime. Permanence is a weighty thing. Impermanence is so much better. We are just here kind of caretaking and you do your caretaking as best as you can while you are here because it's all going to go.

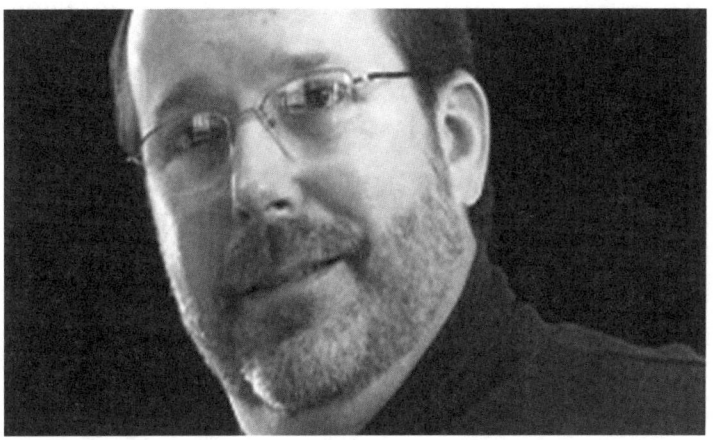

There is something that is permanent and that's creativity.
It's emotion in things we create, be that feelings, be that a piece of art. I don't think that ever goes away. The earth can disappear but I think what you create and you put out there in that universe goes on forever.

I don't think love disappears. That feeling of emotion travels forever. And these feelings go on and can get passed back and forth for generations. They are not objects that we create as human beings that matter. It's the relationships and those feelings that go back and forth between those you love that matter. And that's what's permanent.

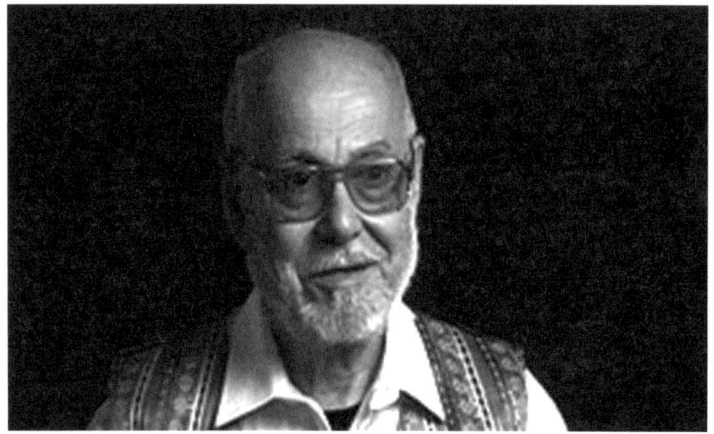

We are permanent in a sense of the whole universe. We are transient in one form. The same elements that are found here in this body, are found some elsewhere. And these elements are not destroyed when this form disappears. They are only transferred to other forms. The conservation of mass, you don't destroy it. It transforms from one face to another.

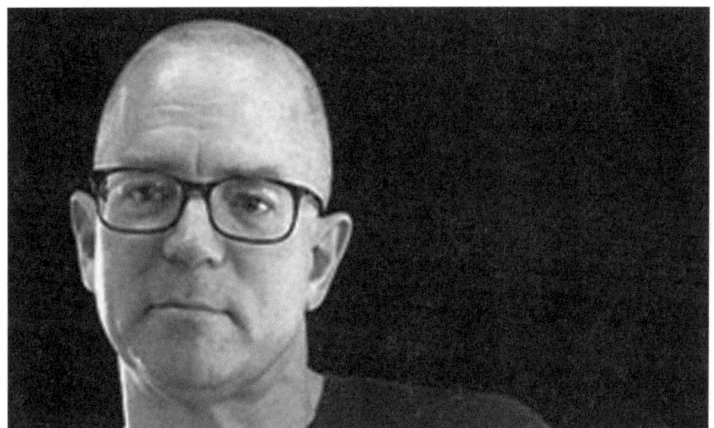

I don't think there's anything that's permanent in the world except the world itself. I think the planet was here a long time before we were here and it will be here a long time after we are gone. It won't be the same but it will be here.

The history of the world, millions of years, it's a speck. What is our planet in the scope of the universe?

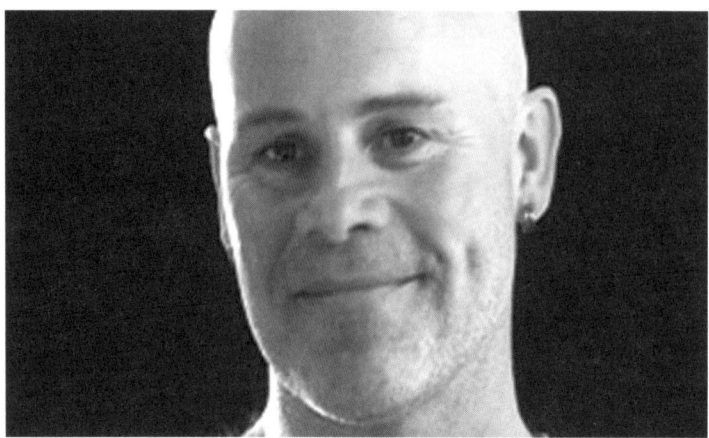

Your sense of what's finite and permanent changes a great deal as you get older. When you are a kid it's impossible to imagine that you'll ever grow old. Old people seem impossibly old to you. It's incomprehensible that you'll ever be that old yourself. Or you won't be around forever.

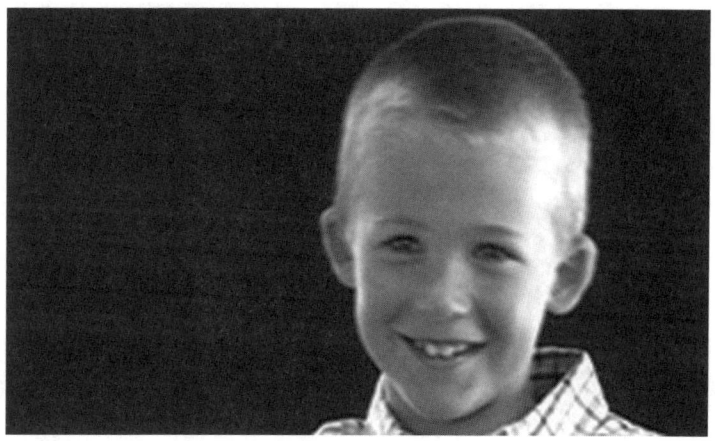

Feelings are permanent. I'll always love my mom.
I'll always love my dad and my sister, even when my sister takes my toys
and breaks them. I still love her.

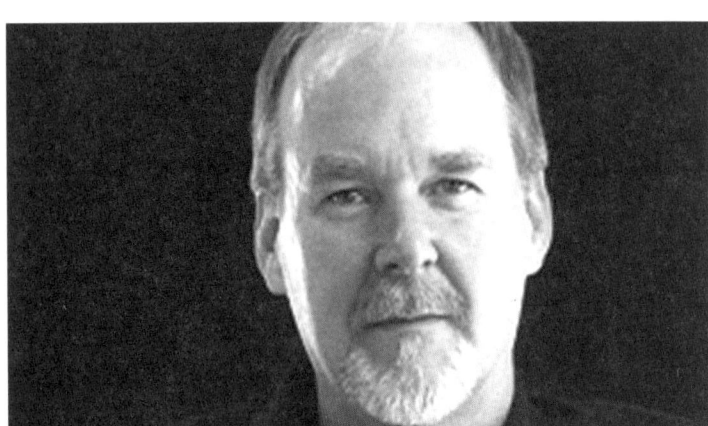

The whole key to this thing is, we are just put in this perception of time. As soon as we drop time, I have a clear sense this moment is permanent. It's not important that I understand how it was before now or how it will be in the future. It just is. It's completely durable and completely permanent to me when I drop time.

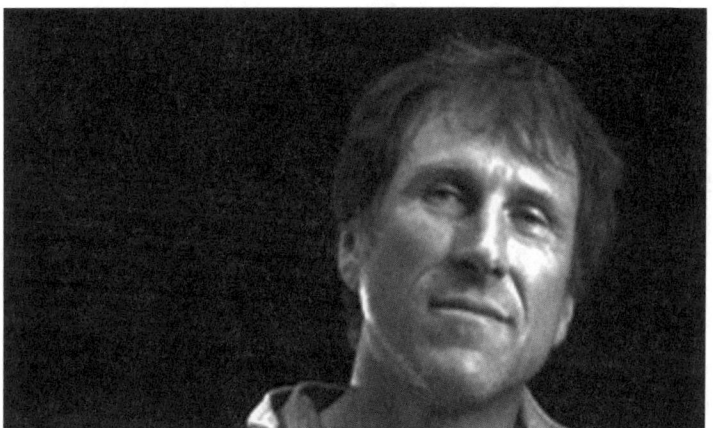

We have to admit impermanence into our lives. It's important to live with impermanence as a frame of reference so that we can approach each moment or each day with a sense of humility about what we are able to do and what we are not able to do and relinquish control over things we cannot have control over. It is important to live as if things are as permanent as stone. You have to invest yourself in love and concern for people, accept people's love as if that's the only thing that exists. The commitment to living as if everything is always there forever with the acceptance that nothing is going to survive.

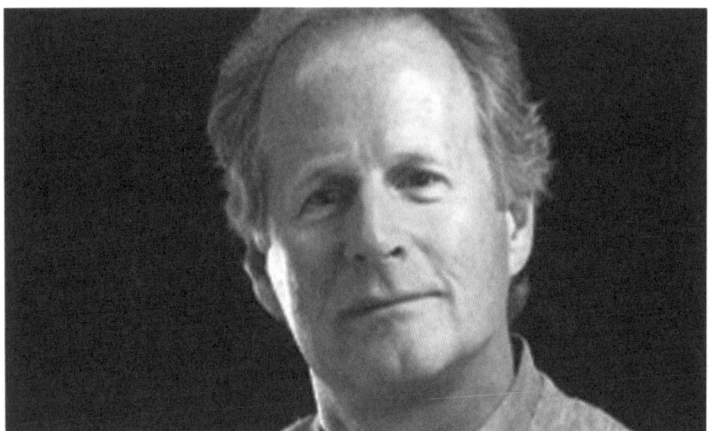

The sense of permanence is more of a human conceptual construct of "what can I hang on to." And when we start hanging on to, our hands close into fists. We try to keep things from moving and keep things from flowing and ultimately try to hold on to some sense of identity that is caught up with illusions of permanence.

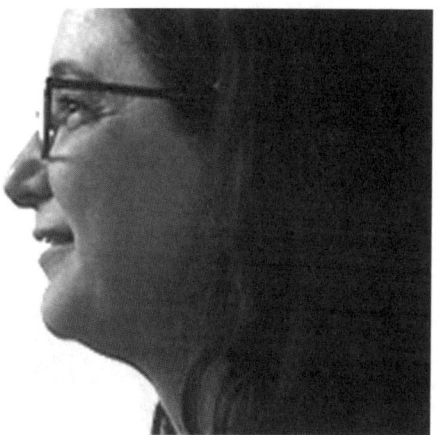

From what I know, life is change so nothing is permanent because it's always in flux and it's always changing. I guess that gives us constant opportunity to learn, to grow, to become more than we are in any given moment.

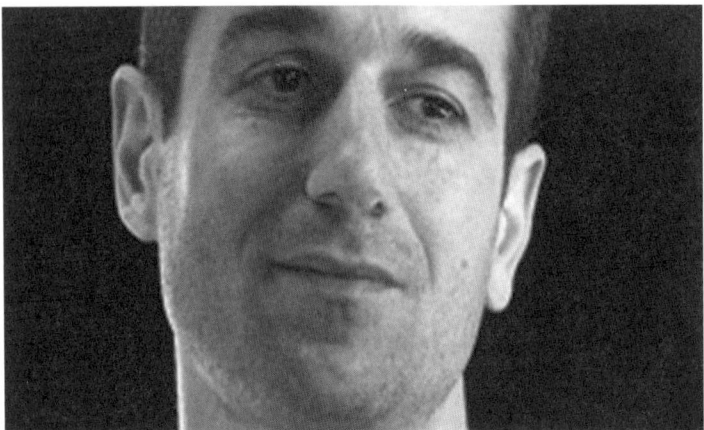

Maybe life itself is a permanent force? There is desire amongst the living to stay alive. Life seems to want to make life and stay living. So that's the life force and that's probably a permanent force.

PEACE

All these conflicts that look so real and so permanent can be muted by just changing the way we look at them.

Shanti, Shanti, Shanti......of Peace, Permanence, and Impermanence
Kavita N. Ramdas

In my language, the word for peace is soothing even in its sounds. *Shanti* is what a mother might whisper to her child. It's a soft shush like the Hebrew *Shalom* and its close relative the Arabic *Salaam*. It is a sound that the ocean makes. What you hear when you listen to a conch shell. It is a quietening—a stilling yet it holds movement within. It is breath, the steady rhythm and unceasing motion that is at once the solid core of all life and something so fleeting, so impermanent, most of us fail to pay it attention on a daily basis.

A breath. Shanti.

A friend of mine died this week. Her breath simply stopped. An asthma attack cut off the air to her lungs and then to her heart. She was 43. A mother of two. The boat that took her ashes out into the Indian Ocean was accompanied by dolphins – somehow they came to be with those who mourned her. Sitting here, far away, with my eyes closed I could see them sharing their message of peace, reminding us of the permanence of love and the impermanence of life.

How does one define peace? In the Upanishads, the philosophical treatises of ancient India, Shanti referred to a state entered into by the soul at rest, where all desires are fulfilled—a peace that passes all understanding. In the Oxford English Dictionary it is described as a sense of freedom from any dissension, quarrels, anxiety, fear or conflict. We speak of being at peace as we speak of being at rest. Or at war.

Yet, the notion of peace simply being the absence of war or conflict has been challenged over the ages by many courageous and compassionate people. In contemporary social movements we speak of a just peace—ensuring the real conditions that make living well possible for all human beings. Recently, Bolivia's President Evo Morales expressed this notion in these words: "Living well, is to not think only in terms of per capita income, but in terms of cultural identity, community, harmony between ourselves and mother earth."

Today our world struggles with the dilemma of how to create conditions of lasting and just peace. We know that to truly succeed in that effort will require us both to face our shared histories of oppression and imperialism and to be willing to challenge current inequalities and imbalances in power. It requires the courage to make amends for past injustice. In grassroots movements around the globe, among the peasants of Chiapas, the women protesting the dam in the Narmada valley in India, the monks standing up to a military junta in Burma or Chinese police in Tibet, there are signs that achieving that Shanti may actually depend on people's ability to create what Martha Graham once described as "blessed unrest." Indeed, for the social movements seeking to free our environment of pollution, make water a human right, and demand adherence to the Geneva conventions, and equality for women and men alike, peace is about making the conscious choice to first imagine and then act to make real a world where there is growth without inequality, wealth without plunder, work without exploitation, and a future without fear.

If, collectively, we aspire towards that understanding of peace as an active commitment to living in friendship and amity not only amongst ourselves as human beings, but also with other life forms and our earth, we may come to recognize that Shanti is closely linked to the principle of Ahmisa. Often translated as "non-harm," Ahimsa is not simply negative non-violence or non-injury. It is a positive cosmic love—an embracing of all life without fear. It is why Gandhi spoke of peace and ahimsa as the ultimate weapon in the struggle for truth.

In my work with women's rights activists worldwide, I have come to better understand the implication of Martin Luther King's famous words, "The arc of the moral universe is long, but it bends toward justice." So, despite its being a movement without formal leaders, without an army, without any formalized leadership structure, I believe the effort to find and realize a "just peace" will indeed prevail. The movement will prevail because of Rashida Bee, a survivor of the ghastly 1984 industrial tragedy in Bhopal, who declared, "We the people, are not flowers offered at an altar of profit and power, but dancing flames committed to conquering darkness and challenging those who threaten the planet and the magic and mystery of life." Author Paul Hawken reminds us it will prevail, "not because it will defeat, conquer or create harm, but because in its myriad forms it offers us a different vision of what is possible if we commit to both ecological and social restoration." The most transformative social movements are effective precisely because they refuse to give up hope that the world might indeed be a kinder and more just place; they are undeterred by obstacles and do not cease their struggle simply because their efforts fail to register immediate measurable gains.

Our hope for a world at peace is not unlike both the remarkable steadfastness and incredible fragility of our own breath and the breath of our complex planet earth. There is reason both to believe and have faith in its resilience, its reliable rhythm, and to be motivated by a sense of urgency and the realization that this moment, this breath, this present, is all that we have.

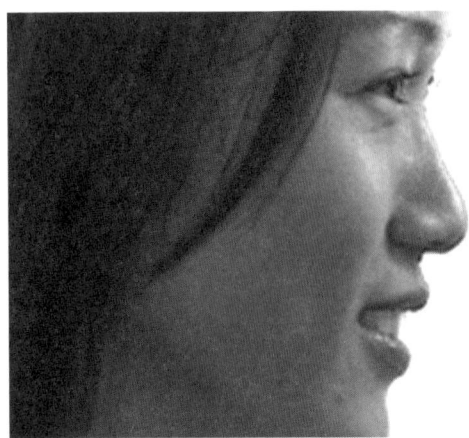

I look at peace differently, and realize peace is not this lofty goal that's hard to get to. Rather, peace is when you get up in the morning and ask, are you at peace with yourself? Are you satisfied with who you are as a person, a child, a parent, a role model, a member of society? I think when you start thinking like that, peace becomes who you are, then I think we will get to peace on a bigger scale.

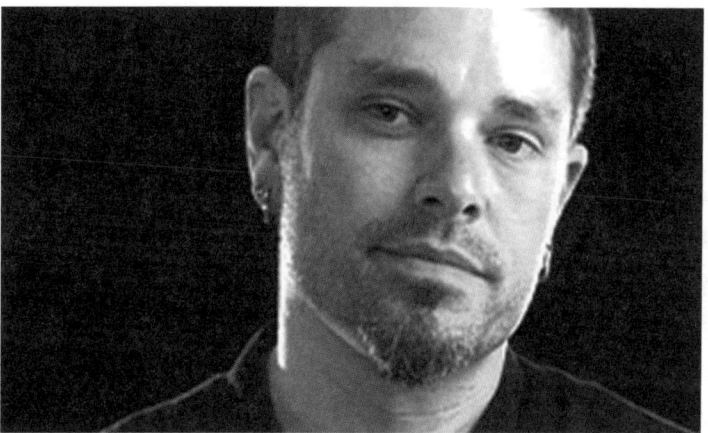

Peace happens in an awareness that nothing is real outside of this moment. The only thing that we have is this moment and it is the only thing that's real. That's where the deepest peace comes when you rest into that. Let go of fear, don't hold on, quiet your mind and come to the moment.

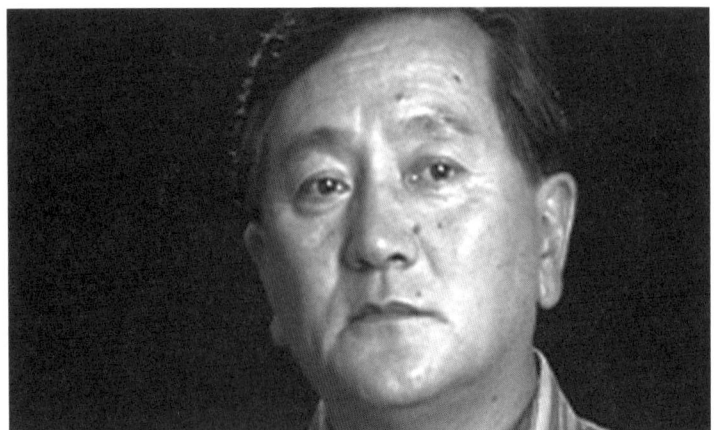

Impermanence might contribute towards greater peace in the world. All these conflicts that look so real and so permanent can be muted by just changing the way we look at them.

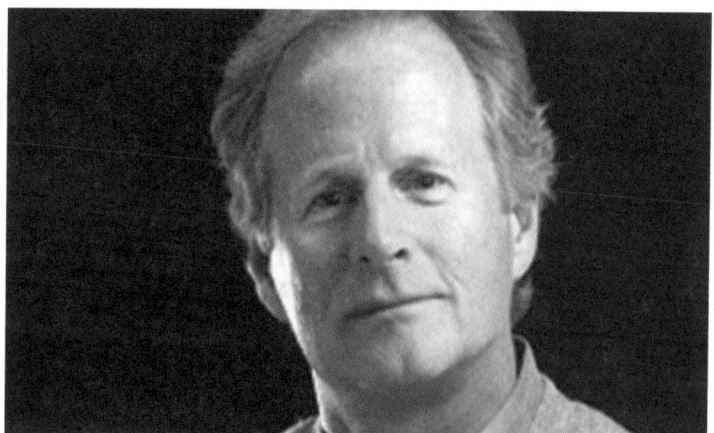

It's been said that "you can't hate someone whose story you really know." The better we know our own story, even spiraling into that infinite permanence, that metaphysical continence at the center, the more we know that, the more we know that's true for everyone. It's the same consciousness, the same energy, the same love that is centering all that seems to have any permanence or impermanence. The more we tune into that, the more we treat anything or anyone from that sense of reverence of being connected in a sacred way.

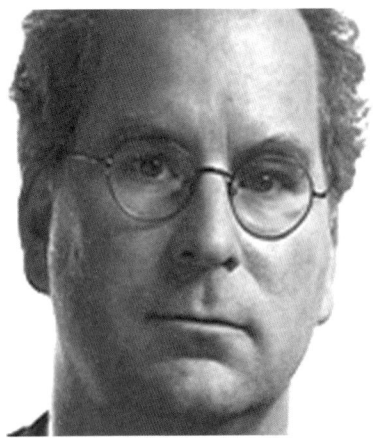

If there's something that can help us towards peace, that I've discovered in my own life, it is to take time to understand the breadth of what people are and the depth. Take time to travel and take time to see what is happening over time. By getting a broader point of view, it becomes more difficult to hate. It becomes much more difficult to think that somebody is an other.

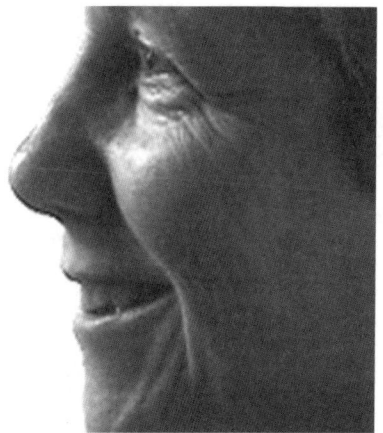

It would be horrible if the world was black and white and if nothing changed. The beauty about people is that every single person is different. The only way we can have world peace is to realize and celebrate the fact that every-one is different and how beautiful that is and it puts color in our world. The world works a lot better when there's a little bit of give and take on all sides.

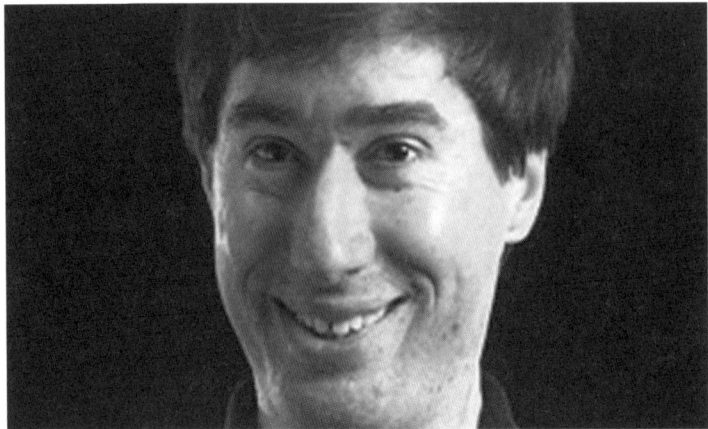

I think we are here to make music. Music is where we all connect because it's the vibration of the universe. It is the dance of the gods. Playing music, you connect with people in a non-symbolic way. It's a direct way. It's beyond language. "Getting in tune" is really about touching the absolute vibration of the universe. If we are all making music, we are all in tune with each other, and we are at peace with each other.

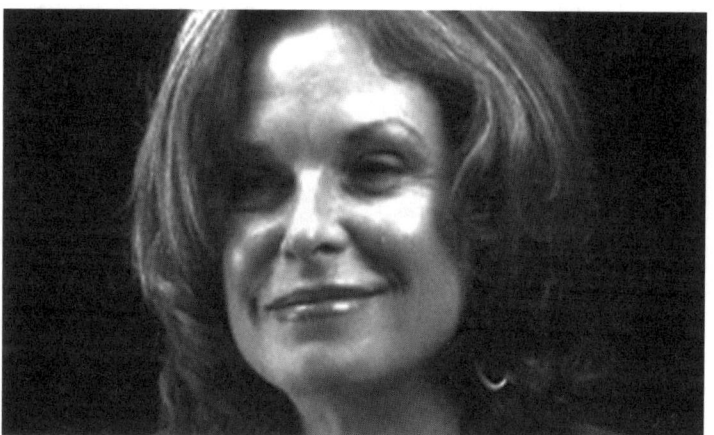

I'm lucky. My profession is to give. It gives a great pleasure when you give to other people and I think that's part of the peace process. It's not about taking, it's about giving it back.

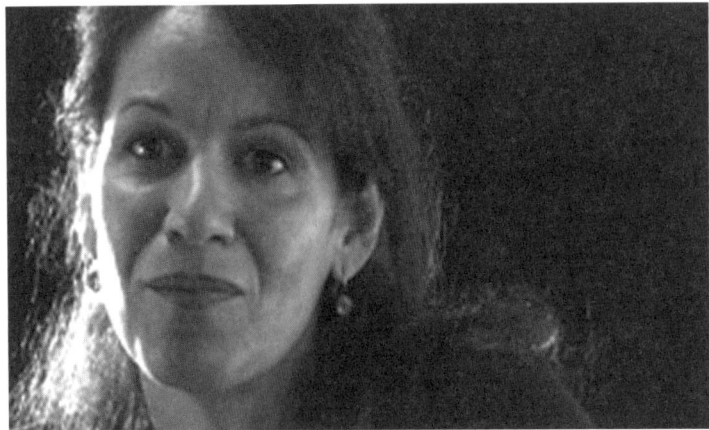

Being in tune with the process of impermanence. Evolving, changing and being open to that lends to an inner peace, it lends to communing with others. When you are open to change and open to seeing from another perspective, it lends to peace.

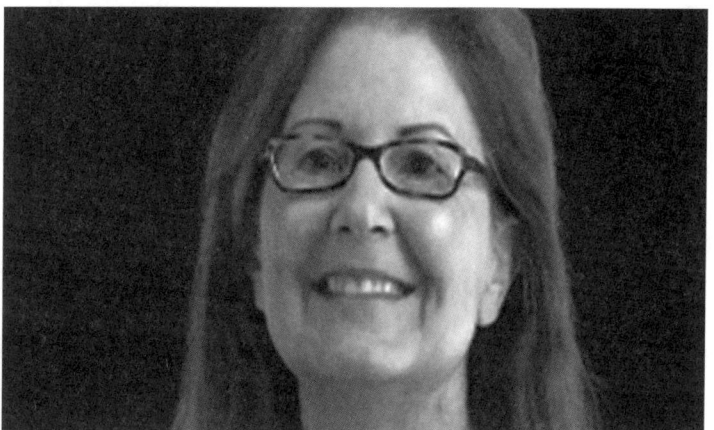

Total peace on earth, I don't think it's possible. I just don't think we have that total control to able to be peaceful animals, peaceful beings. The work that has to be done now is to evolve as persons. Thinking, talking, acting, and understanding the preciousness of life. Understanding the impermanence of life. How we are responsible for peace in the world. It's each of us, one by one by one by one. Collectively, we can make a more peaceful world.

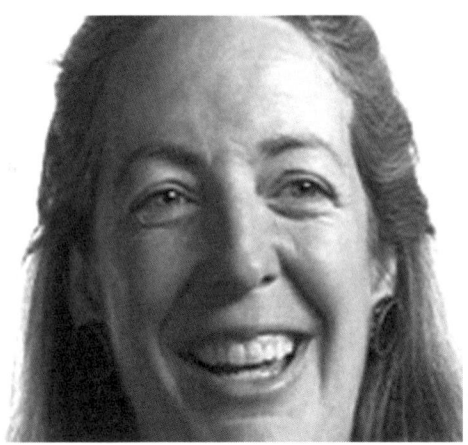

I'm able to keep up the sensibility of change by travel. It's through that constant changing and throwing yourself into an environment where you don't speak the language or you don't speak it very well, or you are unfamiliar with the surroundings. It just kind of keeps you on your toes and makes you more aware.

The world is connected through the internet and if you know people in Afghanistan and Iraq and the Middle East, you might think differently about what you hear in the media about war. I think it's really important get into another culture and start to feel something about others.

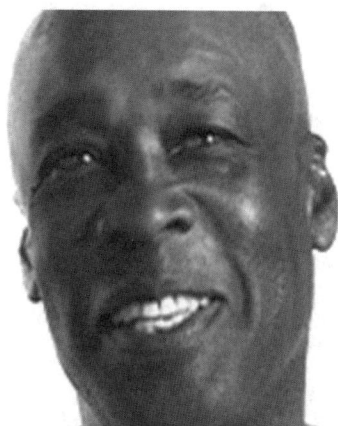

To create a more peaceful world, we should all come together. We've been fighting for something that does not belong to us. This world does not belong to us. We belong to this world. So we should live in this world with love and understand one another.

I have to change it here. What I eat, what I do around me. Then my soul can travel where it belongs. If I don't do those changes nothing else in me is good. I have to keep on loving. I love and respect everyone.

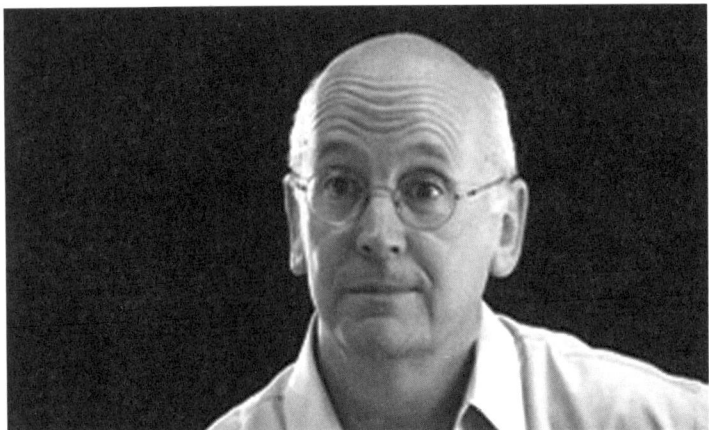

You can't have universal religion but you can have universal spirituality. And the universal spirituality is when we enter into meditation. It's basically the same for all of us. Experientially the fruits of meditation are the same.

The level of dialogue, you are able to respect differences. And the differences are just as important as the similarities and the parallels. Unless you are content with impermanence then you are always looking for final answers that will never change, the formula that is perfect. Through the practice of meditation, you are able to let go of the passing attachments of your mind and recognize how much your consciousness is ephemeral and live with that and let it pass, let it go.

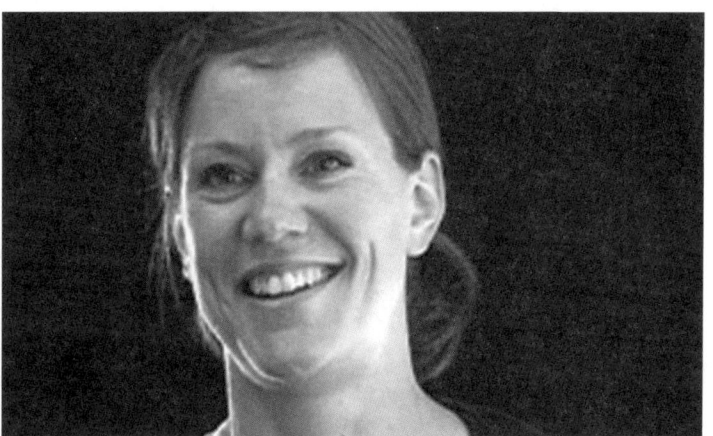

Figure out a way to change without knowing the end. I think that can make you a peaceful person. If you are able to be curious, more open and embrace other people and what they are going through and who they are.

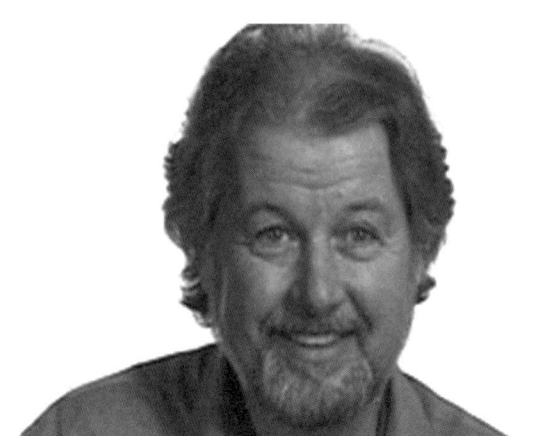

Peace requires as much if not more discipline as war does. So maybe if we can really face our mortality, if we can face our mortality of life, and embrace it, we'd be more willing to share. We'd be more willing to change our lives, change the way we do it for the greater and larger good.

How do we learn to listen to the wisdom of the natural systems? When I go out into the forest, it's the one of the places that I always know I can experience peace.

The fundamental energy that you want with life is respect. Respect for and respect from life, people around you.My ability to really see you and really respect who you are, see the essence of who you are, and to honor and respect that, will allow us to live in peace no matter what circumstances we find ourselves in.

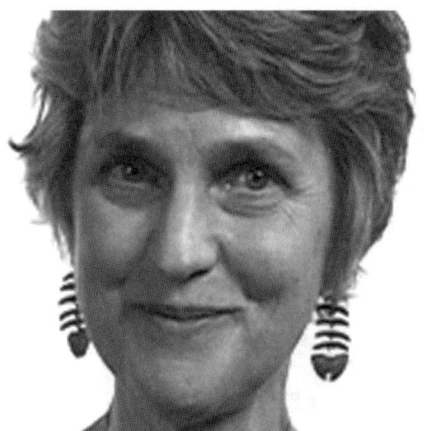

Any kind of peace is impermanent. Peace within myself is impermanent. If it's hard to be peaceful within oneself and that peace is not lasting even on an individual basis, you can imagine how hard it is to create peace between or among many people.

I think the trick is to start inside. It's an inside job. And if an individual can find peace within him or herself and work out from there, I think that's the best hope for the planet. It's the best hope for human beings.

You can't work towards world peace from a place of anger.
You have to work towards world peace by first finding peace within yourself. And that's the hardest thing of all. I'm still working on it.

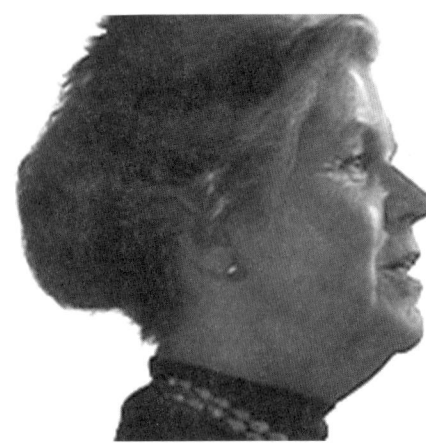

I believe that war is part of the human evolutionary journey of learning. And that we have reached the limits of what we can teach us and it's time to transcend war. It's the human journey of learning.

Making our way back to the remembrance that we are all one. That we truly are one. Not just one as humans but one with all of life.

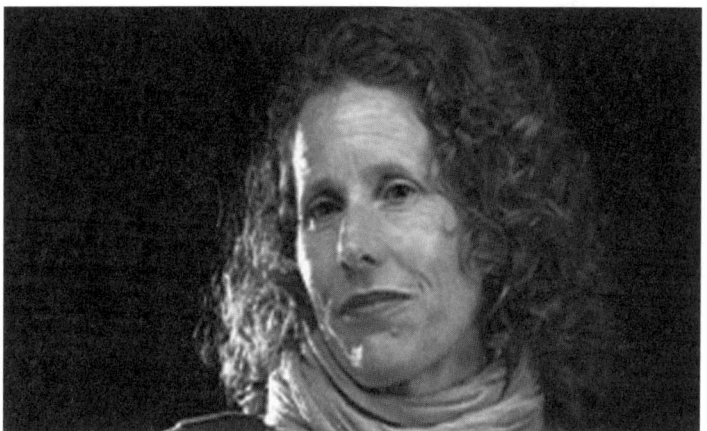

One way of creating peace is starting within ourselves. If we don't start inside, it can't be expressed outwardly.

You can look at somebody just walking along and you might look at that person and smile and that could affect their whole day. A smile, the energy that comes from that can be very healing to someone even though you don't know them.

I hope for myself that's something I can remember every single day and I have to remind myself all the time because I believe that there's a lot of power in that. Our thoughts and our words carry a lot of energy. We have some responsibilities to the way that we think and speak and that can effect peace in the world. Because thoughts are very powerful, thoughts carry energy.

LAST DAY

If today was the last day, then I'm just as grateful as I was yesterday as I will be tomorrow when I don't exist.

Last Days
Philip A. Pizzo, M.D.

At some level we each have personal experiences, perceptions, understandings and reactions about the beginning and the end of life. Most of us are more comfortable reflecting on life's inception than on death and dying. While we recognize that our own deaths are inevitable, most of us think little about our last days. When we do, our images are shaped by our fears and hopes, our perceptions of reality and our denial of that reality, our understandings of the worldly and the spiritual, and our expectations about whether death will be an ending or a new beginning.

My perceptions of death and last days have been shaped by nearly four decades as a physician, the majority of which has been spent caring for children with catastrophic diseases like cancer and AIDS. As a pediatrician I have witnessed and rejoiced at life's beginnings. While it is true that most children are born to live, I have all too frequently watched children, teenagers and young adults face the prospect of their last days well before they have had a full measure of life.

When I began my work as a pediatric oncologist I was taught—and initially believed—that the one thing I could promise a child and parent facing a catastrophic disease was that the transition from life to death could be made comfortable—or at least without pain and suffering. And while I have marveled at the progress that has been made in averting death from cancer and other catastrophic diseases, and in improving supportive and palliative care, I have still experienced all too often the failure of medical treatment to conquer disease or to provide dignity to the transition from life to death. The spectrum is wide and includes the child who is able to experience a last day in a parent's arms to those whose death occurs in ways that distance or frighten both the child and the family. While some take comfort from deeply held religious convictions about the inevitability of death, and the belief that suffering will be followed by an afterlife in which there is no pain, all who experience the death of a child suffer some consequences. Future memories, feelings and even beliefs are never left unchanged when one lives through the last day of a child. My feelings and beliefs have been affected over and over again by such experiences.

Over time physicians learn to compartmentalize their emotions, especially when caring for children with life-threatening disease. And while I have learned to do this to varying extents, I have never permitted myself to be distant from the emotional reaction to a child's suffering or death, believing that doing so would make me a less compassionate and caring physician. I have sat by the bedside of innumerable dying children, held their hands and those of their parents, felt and tried to ease their pain, and, in a number of cases, with their parents' understanding and sometimes urging, helped ease their discomfort even while it accelerated their child's demise.

I have had candid and frank discussions with children about their last days—some of whom were barely old enough to read. Children have remarkable insight into their inner being; unshackled or unbiased by life's experiences or expectations, they can be remarkably honest and perceptive. Most children also feel a need to protect their parents and nearly all know, at some level, when their own last day is imminent. While it is obvious that nearly all children are oriented toward living, and can do remarkable things even when impaired by illness and suffering, it is also true that children sense when their own death is imminent. I have witnessed youngsters who described dreams about angels coming to help them to "heaven" and others whose pain and suffering seemed to preempt their ability to achieve emotional or physical solace and just wanted to "be gone." Sometimes the accommodation to a child's last day occurs suddenly and other times it takes place over months or even years—with rising and ebbing emotional intersections with the inevitable, the finite, the ending.

There is no question that my view of life has been dramatically altered through experiencing the last days of children. When I was caring for children during the early days of the AIDS outbreak in the US, watching dozens of children and teenagers suffer the hopelessness of life or last days marred by pain, difficulty breathing, and deterioration of the motor or cognitive functions, I found myself increasingly angry at the unfairness of a disease to which I could not reconcile myself—and initially could not reverse or even treat. My personal moments of inner silence were rapidly supplanted, even invaded, by visions of children suffering unfairly and reaching the end of life before they had experienced its awakening—and of the suffering of their families. While I am not a religious person, I have always felt a spiritual domain—although not accompanied by a belief in an afterlife, reincarnation or even the existence of a soul. But any sense of spirituality can be challenged by images of last days that come too soon or seem to occur without justice or reason.

And while over time I have put some of these feelings into perspective, there can be do doubt that the view of my own inevitable last days is affected by those I have witnessed in the children and families I have cared for as a doctor. They impact the way I wish or hope I might manage or assist in the last days of my loved ones—or of those I experience myself. I have long believed that when there is a chance for life—and one that embraces quality and dignity—every effort should be made to secure and salvage it. But I have also come to believe that when that chance is slim to nonexistent, or when the suffering exceeds the value of living, those last days should be accelerated and the transition from life to death made with greater dignity—physically and spiritually.

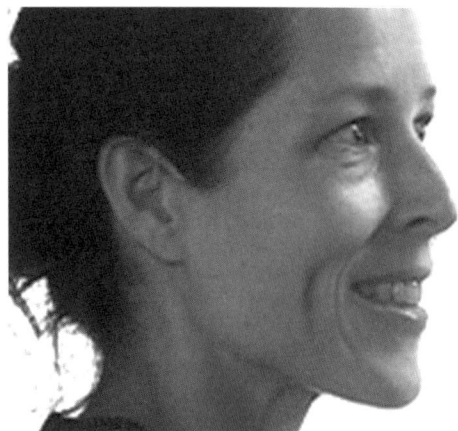

I don't think the last day is as important as all the days beforehand. It's definitely your day-to-day that matters and your moment-to-moment and what you put out. So your last day, your last moment you get to face your life, I think it's going to be really quick and not very important.

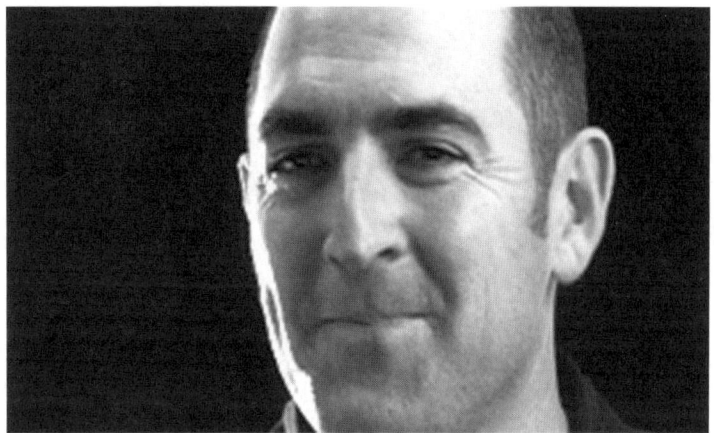

Through my twenties and thirties, I felt like I tried to run fast and try to get somewhere. The last few years, I felt like I'm not trying to run as fast.
It is what it is. In many ways, it's uncontrollable.

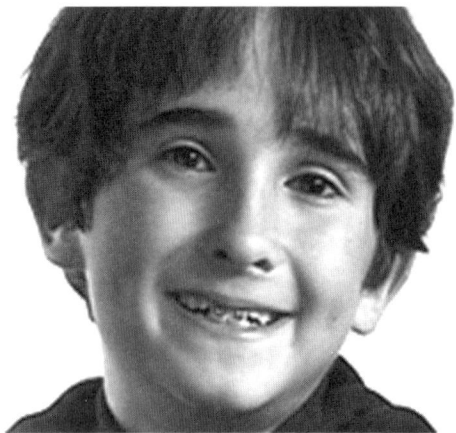

I'm not scared of death and I wouldn't be scared of it because I plan to live a long, long life. If I plan to do that, I am most likely to have a long life.
If you believe in having something, you probably will so I'm thinking of having a long life and I want to live long. I probably will have a long life because that's what I want to do.

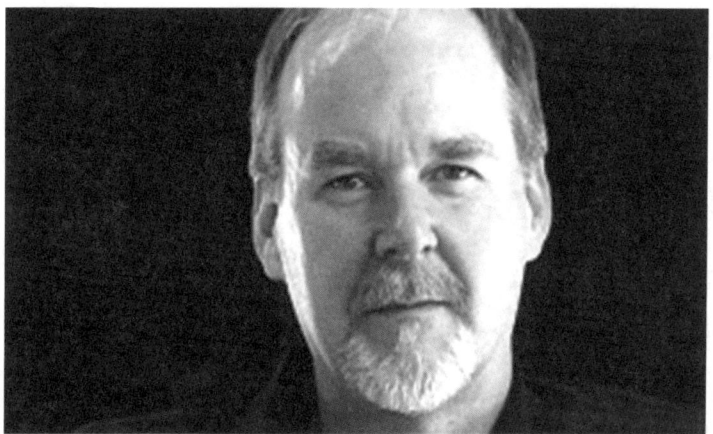

If today was the last day of the life of this body, it's fine. It's only the last day of the way I'm put together in this particular way. It's only the last day in the construct of time. Throw away time, and throw away attachments to this particular assembly of atoms, then it's not the last day.

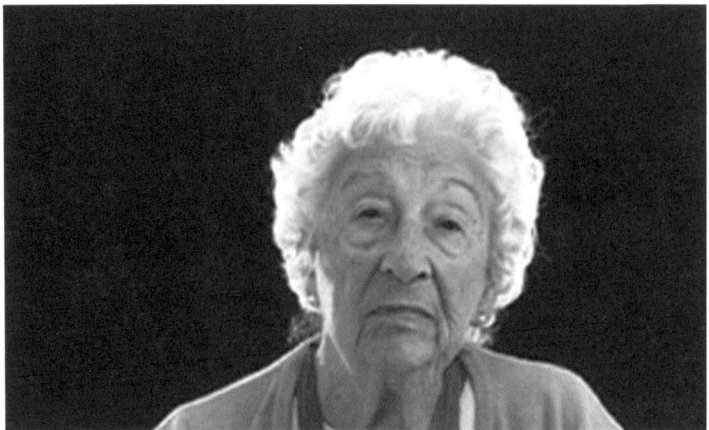

At my age, I'm ready to go to my maker. You know it's going to happen someday but I'm going to keep on living until I die.

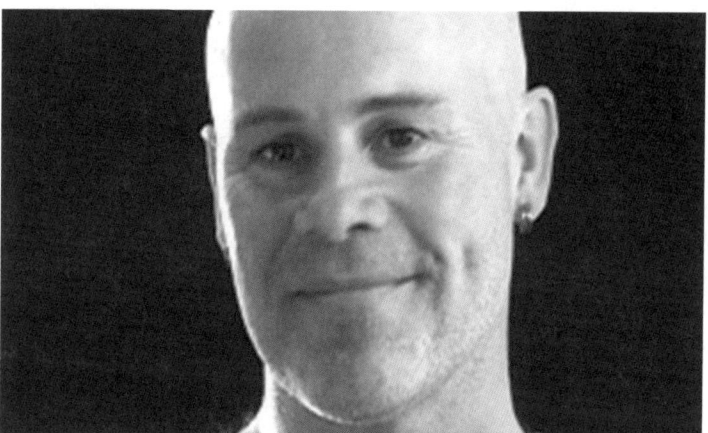

There's not much that I would need to get done before the sun went down if today was the last day. Mainly, I would want to get in touch with people that are important to me. I think it would be about people, not really about things or about experiences. Let them know how important it was that they were part of my existence.

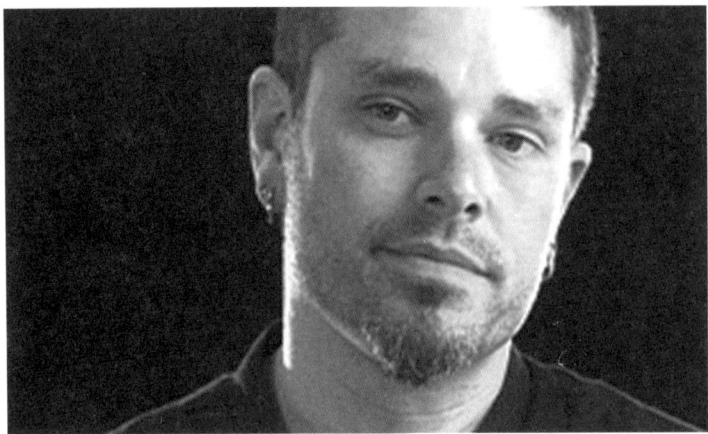

If today was the last day of my life, I would be afraid. I would long for things that I imagined I would do. I would long for the dreams of the future.

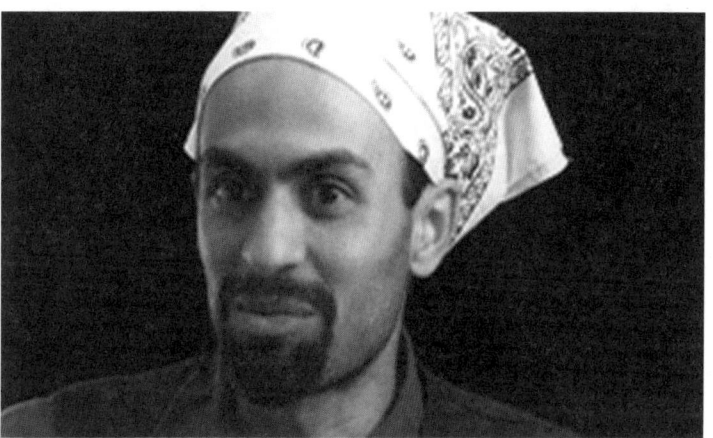

If today was the last day, then I'm just as grateful as I was yesterday as I will be tomorrow when I don't exist.

PERISH & FLOURISH

There's a need for something to perish in order for life to begin new.

Flourish and perish—time is US
Mihai Nadin

    The manor looked impressive. Every detail—from the flower beds to the birdhouses, from the window decorations to the doorknobs, from the immaculate pebble road leading to the entrance, to the impressive chimneys without a crack—testified to assiduous maintenance. Trees aged as time passed, but were trimmed to look the same year after year. Each new season was marked with flowers in full bloom. Spent blossoms were replaced so quickly that the flowers seemed never to die.

    Not far away, in a clearing in the woods, a smaller dwelling, almost impossible to notice from the road, seemed to avoid the embarrassment of comparisons. Although the same age as the manor, the little house aged, as everything in this world does. Life insinuated itself in the moss-covered stones around the foundation. A stork made its nest on the chimney. Flowers gave in to new seasons. From winter to spring, dead leaves blanketed the grounds. New plants, with different colors and shapes, grew through what had gently perished, as though to make place for what was yet to flourish.

    As the years went by, neither the owner of the manor nor the owner of the little house hidden among the trees could do anything to hold back time from showing on themselves: one, obsessed with perfection, in which he saw a way to stop time; the other, happy to ride on the river of life, never failing to be amazed by what he saw and heard and felt. Nothing the same, nothing repeated, so much left behind. So much still ahead.

    As stories want events to go, the owner of the manor got bored one day—why on that particular day, after so many decades, no one knows—and finding nothing to perfect in his timeless world, took a walk beyond its grounds. Before he knew it, he reached his neighbor's house. Nothing here conformed to his sense of order. He could have turned back, but something made him linger. Finally he went to the door and knocked. The man who answered seemed surprised. He did not ask his visitor, "Are you still alive?" but this is what he could not help thinking. Indeed, every time his head turned towards the manor, he wondered if there was any life to it, since the beauty of the place stayed the same. The man living there looked like a portrait of himself—stiff, ageless, seeming no more real than the paint that impressed his likeness on the taut canvas.

    "Why is your place in such disgusting shape? The wood is rotting. The bricks are splitting. Look at the roof! Moss is growing on top of it. And look at the trees, the branches never pruned and growing every which way! And do you call these weeds flowers?" He pointed to some unrecognizable flower whose petals, pulled by the breeze, were slowly falling to the ground, leaving stalks, topped by half-full pods, and withering leaves behind.

    The owner of the home in the woods was surprised. Where his neighbor saw rot and decline, his eyes—probably less sharp than at the time of their first meeting—recognized the rhythm of life. Those flowers, which his neighbor wanted as perfect and ever-blooming as those at his castle, gave the entire place a sweet perfume, and a sense of fragility. But he did not want to argue. His neighbor seemingly did not realize that whatever did not change was no longer alive.

    They sat, on the chairs he had made some many years ago, which now wobbled as weight was put on them. A bird flew out of the nest it had hidden between beams. A spider retired to the middle of its web. They could hear a softly babbling brook some-where in the woods. A fly buzzed overhead, and in the distance, unseen, some birds kept calling to each other.

    "Next time you walk by the castle, stop in," the guest said, almost as if asking for a favor.

    "Why not? Looks nice. So many people stop in front of it and admire it."

    "Do you admire it?"

"This is my place. And I like to think of it as part of me. There is nothing here that I didn't make myself. Some things are wearing out, breaking down, falling apart. But they're still as full of life as I am."

"The castle is my place. And until the end of time, it will stay as beautiful as it is now. People will look at it and remember me."

"Will they?"

The question remained unanswered. The visitor departed, as impatient as he was when he knocked at the door. Days passed, and, again to his surprise, the owner of the modest house in the woods opened the door to his neighbor.

"'Will they remember me?' you asked, and since then, I've had no peace of mind. I was sure they would. But after seeing your place, I realized that I can see you, and only you, in everything that's here. Even in this flower," to which he pointed.

"Does that surprise you?"

"Yes! You give your own life to all you do. You flourish and decline, and flourish again, in all that you've done." The flower he kept glancing at seemed to say the same thing. "This flower is beautiful."

"All flowers are beautiful."

"How come mine are not as alive as yours?"

"Did you give them life?"

He was taken aback, but then retorted, "What do you mean? I ask the gardeners what to plant and show them where to plant." They looked at each other in the eye.

"Here is a shovel, and here are some seeds. Have a try."

"But I don't know how. I've never done this before.

"Just try."

Not really convinced, he tried anyway. Later he left, carried by his doubts back to the place of his certitudes. Next spring, a little plant bravely made its appearance through the soil. As he cleared around it, and watered it, it was becoming his own. Each day, he returned, afraid that the plant might not make it. Will it get enough water? Sun? Will some insect eat its leaves? More days went by; the first buds opened. He was no longer so sure that he wanted to get back to the gardens at his manor.

And as it is with all there is, after his plant bloomed, the flower eventually dropped its petals, and its leaves yellowed and withered—but not without leaving behind the promise of coming back, in some other ways, embodied in other leaves, other flowers. And through this promise, he himself reconnected to time, from which he was running away almost all his life without even knowing it.

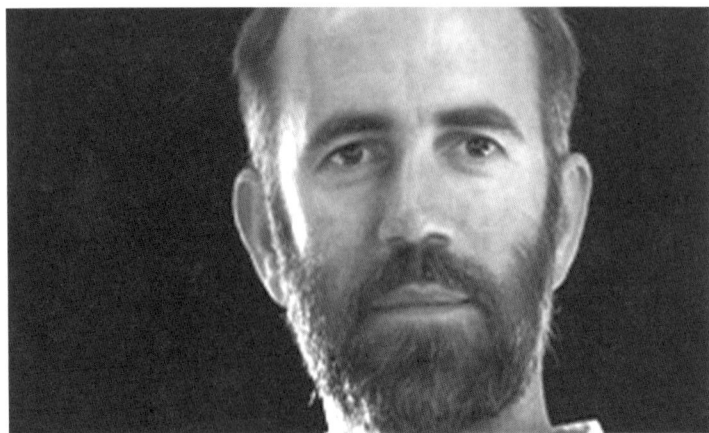

Something has to perish for something else to grow. It could be a habit, a skill, an understanding, a relationship. So I'm going to let go of an old some-thing, an existing something, and by letting go, I'd personally equate that to "it" perishing when that thought, that idea, that habit, that style has perished, it makes room for something else to flourish.

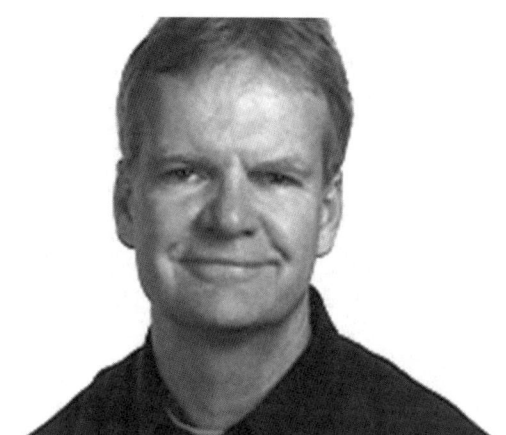

My father passed away about six weeks ago. He was dying of lung cancer. We were very close and on his last night, there was this moment that I will hold on to as long as I'll live. The moment was just holding on to him and there was this deep sense of connection. That hug was just there and it was gone. And yet, there's this eternity of gift that I will carry with me.

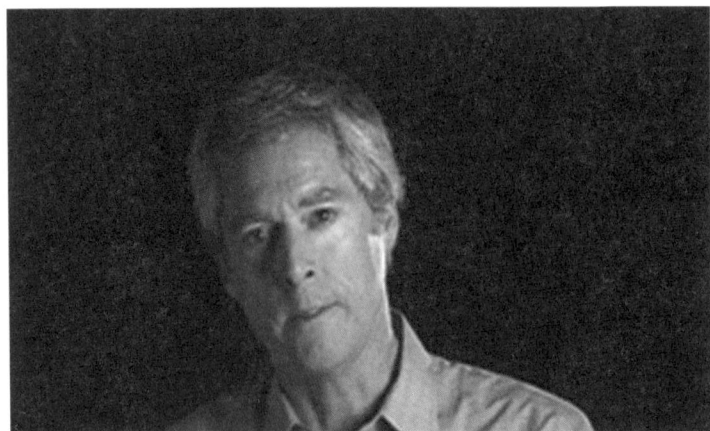

There's a type of serenity, type of calm, type of lack of anxiety that flourishes in one's heart. An awareness that I can flourish in the midst of the changes in human relationship, the changes in my own body as I age, the changes in location, occupation, the changes in health. I have some awareness, some type of vision, appreciation, it's possible to flourish in the midst of that and even a vision, it's possible to perish and flourish at the same time.

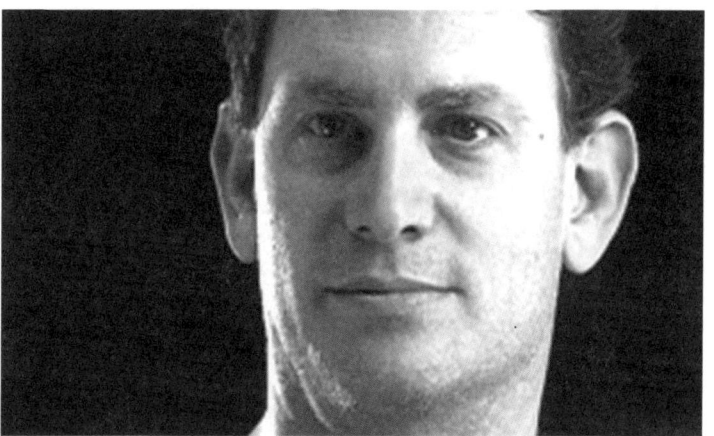

While you move away from something, something else is going to take its place. Fires wiping out forest to recreate a forest. There's a need for something to perish in order for life to begin new. One generation giving up what it had offered, allowing the next generation to have its moment.

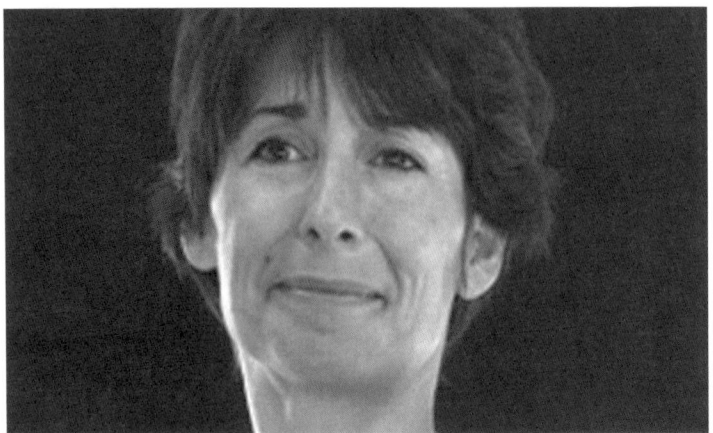

It makes me think of the residue of what would be left behind if somebody is able to flourish and perish at the same time. We are actually doing that already because we are constantly in the dying process. And the residue that is left behind is positive.

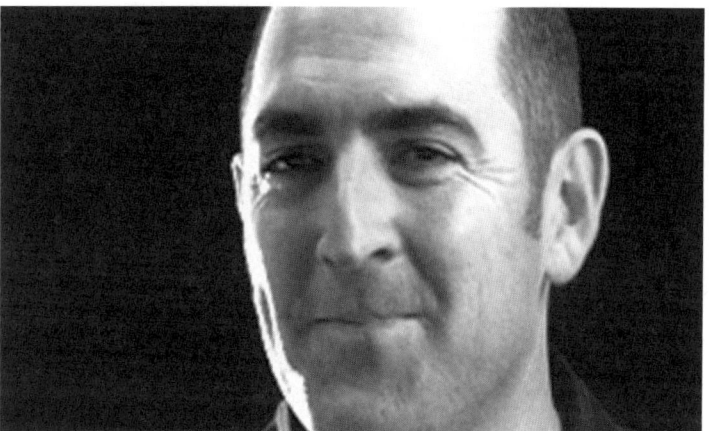

I believe that my dad is perished and flourishes within me. My kids never met my dad. He was a woodworker and I give them things that he made. I think he is flourishing today. Whether he is flourishing or his spirit is flourishing, I have no idea. He lives with us. And I think the same would be true for myself. I would hope that I would flourish.

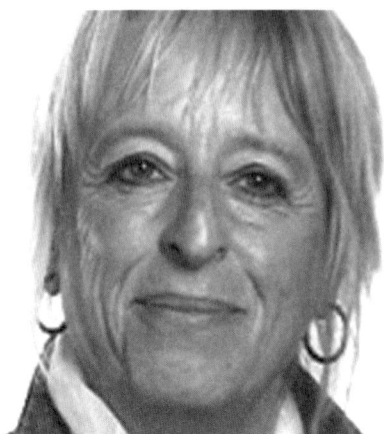

As a basket maker, my trade embodies a lot of that sense of life and death and rebirth. The fibers that I'm using for my basket were living plants. Because of the nature of nature, it also embodies that notion of decomposition and going back to the earth. Basketry is more cyclical in the sense that when I create a piece, I have in my mind that this piece will return to earth someday.

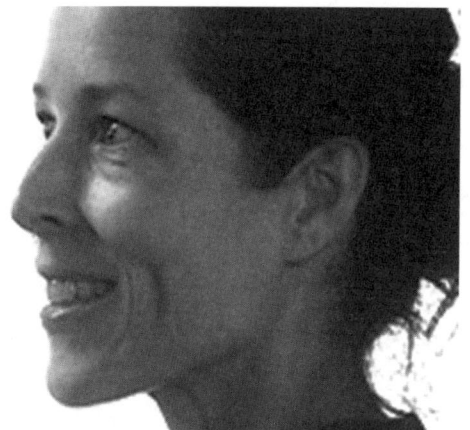

In my relationships, my marriage, it feels that way every cycle when your relationships go into a death period and you revitalize it, make life out of it so I turn to the idea of life coming from death all the time.

MESSAGE TO THE WORLD

If there is going to be any value to any of our lives in the finite period in which we live, it has to come from engaging life. Everybody has an impact.

My Message to the World
Anne Firth Murray

I appreciate being asked to write this essay, "My Message to the World," and it strikes me that, in this time of the internet, all of us can send a message to the world. Therefore, my first thought is to challenge you, dear readers, to think of what your message to the world could be. If you were asked to write such an essay, what would you say?

When I asked a couple of friends, both in their nineties, what their messages to the world would be, they both said this: "Stay alive." I take this to mean that we not only should remain as healthy as possible in order to live, love, and learn over many decades, but we should also "stay alive" in the sense of the way we view the world. I am reminded of this thought: "There are two kinds of people: those who are alive and those who are afraid." Keeping this in mind, "staying alive" means not being afraid, living life fully. Being afraid, which is sometimes inevitable, of course, deadens us. Fear cuts off life. It does not permit us to truly love, to appreciate the beauty of the world, to reach out to help those in need, and to ask for help ourselves.

My message to the world, therefore, would certainly include exhorting you to be alive and unafraid enough to truly love—to be there for others and for the earth, to love beauty, and to be unafraid to work for social justice. One of my first hopes would be that all who live on this earth should have the chance to stay alive, living without fear, living creatively, and being buoyed by the expectancy of old age and love.

In its present state, our world offers no such prospect, and there are forces within it that bedevil the efforts of billions to stay alive. Throughout history the world has suffered at the hands of evil men, and it is suffering now from those who allow evil to be done. Our planet is not a safe place, for the violence of nature is still at work. And its dangers are compounded by the violence of humankind. Vast numbers of women and other marginalized people suffer violence, degradation, and disempowerment, living with fear for their physical safety and their very lives. Until such violence is stopped, there is little hope of a world that offers anything other than a future fraught with danger and fear for many of us. Injustice and violence to one another and to our planet are only two of the issues that seem insurmountable, especially if we think globally. Even in local communities, we seem beset with problems—destructive behavior, environmental degradation—that can make us fearful and therefore not well able to make a difference.

Our shock and sadness about the state of the world or even everyday problems, however, signals our recognition that things can be different. Change can happen. Hope persists. Recognizing a problem and feeling that things can be better is the beginning of change itself. If you have dreamed and hoped, you can be part of the change; you can develop a vision and a plan of action. Gandhi wrote that "we must be the change we wish to see," and I agree. We must embody the change itself, and we must be unafraid to dream of positive change and act on it for the sake of the world.

I write from personal experience. In 1987, I began to dream of creating an organization that would help women around the world be strengthened and empowered. The idea became a passion, and I worked over ten years to put together the Global Fund for Women, which grew from the seed of an idea to a fully developed organization, now the largest foundation in the world working to support the human rights of women. From a dream came a reality.

In the course of developing the Global Fund for Women, I came to know that the way an organization does its work is more important than what it does. And the way we live our lives is more important than what we do. I also learned that there can be some definable steps toward effecting change. First you must dare to dream of positive change and then try to be as clear as possible about what you hope to do and why. As you dream of creating something that will change the world, people may suggest that you are being unrealistically idealistic. Never mind; that may be a good thing. Major change seldom occurs without seemingly unrealistic ideas.

Just dreaming is not enough, however. We need action. A Baha'I philosopher wrote: "What profit is there in agreeing that universal friendship is good, and talking of the solidarity of the human race as a grand ideal? Unless these thoughts are translated into the world of action, they are useless." In other words, as you seek to make positive change, you need to take action to give reality to your dream.

As you begin to realize your dream, think not only of what you want to do but also of the way you want to do it. What is the nature of the program that you want to build? Do you want it to be innovative? If so, seek out people different from yourself to ensure that they will bring in perspectives that you will not imagine. Do you want it to be a calm and gentle place? If so, think of ways that your group can create processes that allow people to feel safe and calm. Are you working on issues of social justice? If so, be sure that all members of the group recognize and respect differences and that the day-to-day activities are based on respect, trust, and compassion. The medium is the message: the way you do your work is more important than what you do.

There are those among us who can be there for others largely because we have the good fortune to live without persistent violence. We need to be fearless in our actions on behalf of others who may need and seek our help. There are others among us who are in pain and need help. They must be fearless in their ability to ask for help as others fearlessly respond. The four mantras on true love of Thich Nhat Hanh come to mind: "Dear One, I am here for you." "Dear One, I know that you are here, and it makes me very happy." "Dear One, I know that you are suffering, and that is why I am here for you." "Dear One, I am in pain; please help."

Mary Oliver asks in her poem "The Summer Day": "Tell me, what is it you plan to do with your one wild and precious life?" Our answers to that question should be our messages to the world.

Here is what I plan to do: Stay alive. Say "yes" to life. Savor the beauties of the world. Believe that change is possible. Make injustice visible and overcome it. Prevent violence. Live without fear. Be there for others. Delight in poetry. Learn. Practice true love.

What about you?

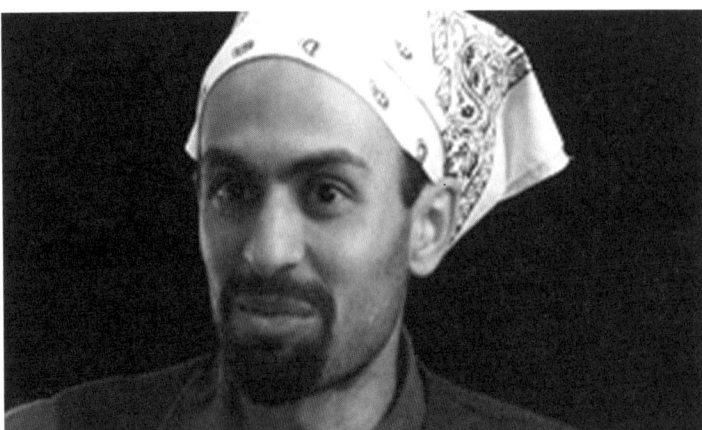

Our existence with these other beings or sharing space is finite. This whole life is a movie, that doesn't just mean that it's my movie and it's for me. It's for all of us.

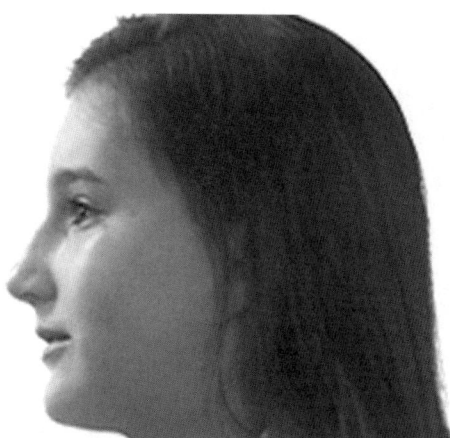

Whatever your age is, you should always think about impermanence and realize how lucky you are. Appreciate what you have and be thankful. Set a good example for everybody. Live every day as if you are going to die tomorrow. Just try to live your life to your fullest and do your best at that.

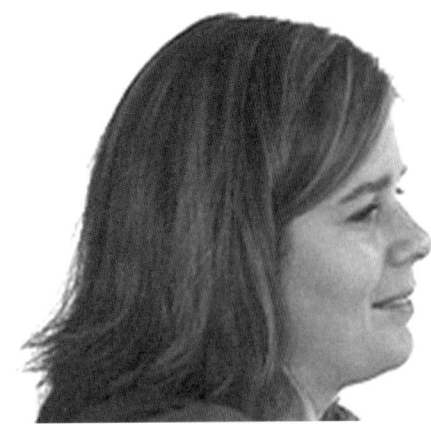

The more accepting people can be of others around them, obviously the more peaceful it's going to be. There's room for everybody's ideas. Accept others' ideas as being as valid as their own. Understand that there are not only people but earth and space, that there are grander needs to be taken care of, there needs to be some energy put into that. People need to act for someone other than themselves.

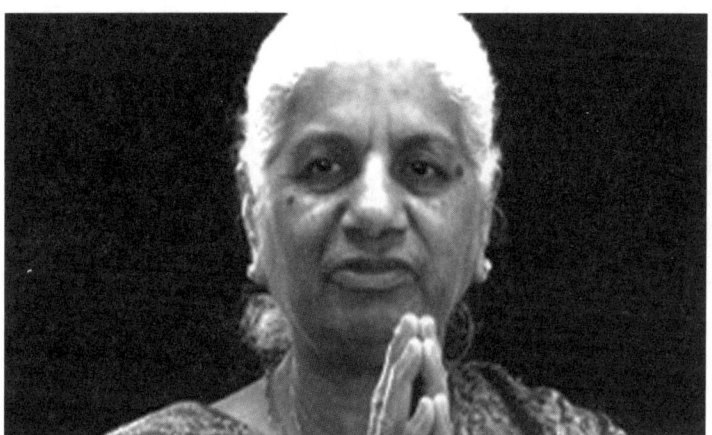

This body is changeable, it is changing constantly moment to moment and the world doesn't remain the same. But our soul is permanent and we have to make a balance between the two. Anger, greed, attachment, selfish attitude, our competition with others, all these things are impermanent features of us. The person who has control of his senses, of his impermanent self, then he can become a pure self and from there, he works selflessly, then we will be in good shape and we will be peaceful.

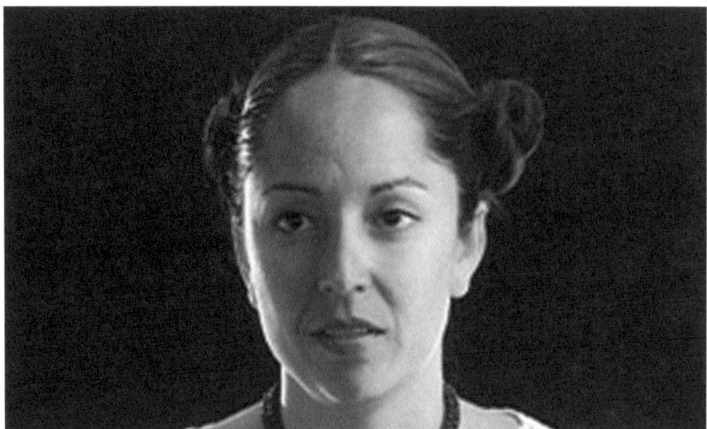

We need to value change. On a personal level, forgiveness is a daily practice. From forgiving yourself to forgiving those around you, to forgiving world
leaders. I think we need to look beyond the material possessions and truly
understand that they are impermanent.

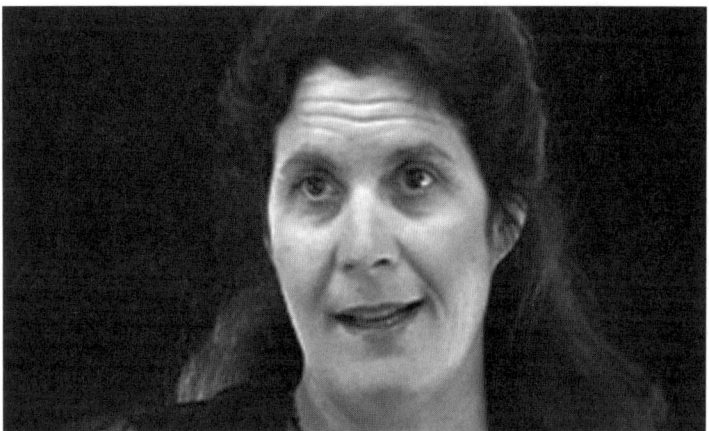

I would want to have everybody work on their fear a little bit. Know that our worry is worthless even though it's hard to turn off. I'm not sure how you let go of the fear but we've got to try.

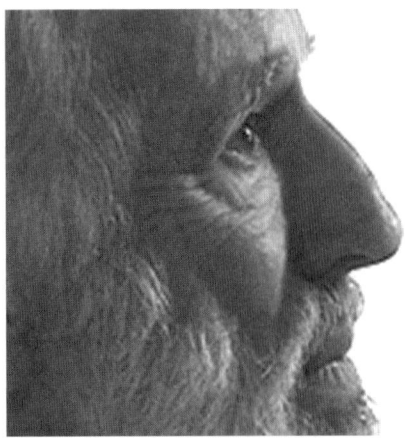

With impermanence being implicit in all of life then you are destined to be creators or within the creative flow. What I feel very passionate about is what our role here on this planet is. I feel it is to be a conscious co-creator.

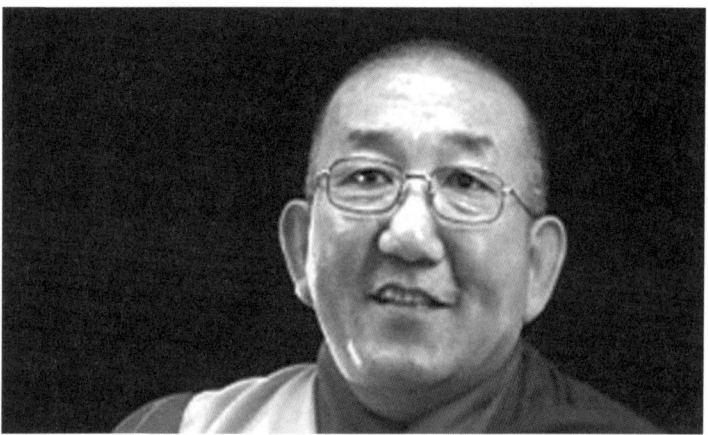

Look at our life as if we are performing opera all day. We should copy some good stories from our history which are compassion, wisdom, harmony, cooperation. If we have these put into our life stories to perform, then the life will be beautiful. Generating compassion is the hardest thing. Compassion is the foundation and once you have compassion, everything is fine.

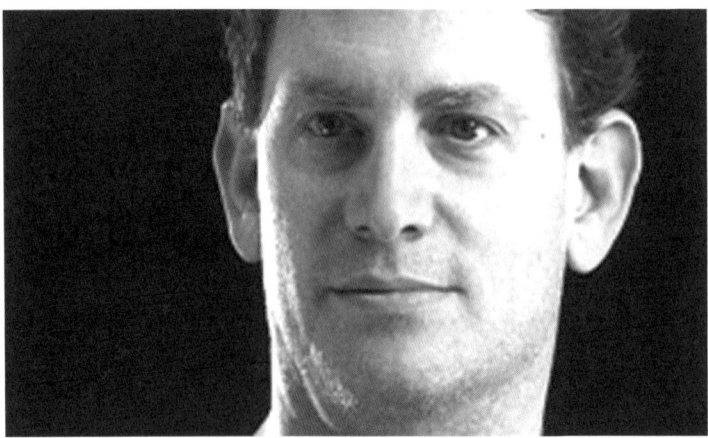

If there is going to be any value to any of our lives in the finite period in which we live, it has to come from engaging life. Everybody has an impact. There are plenty more opportunities to make more impact down the road. Think more broadly, be part of things that are bigger. By engaging little things, you take too much energy away from engaging the bigger things.

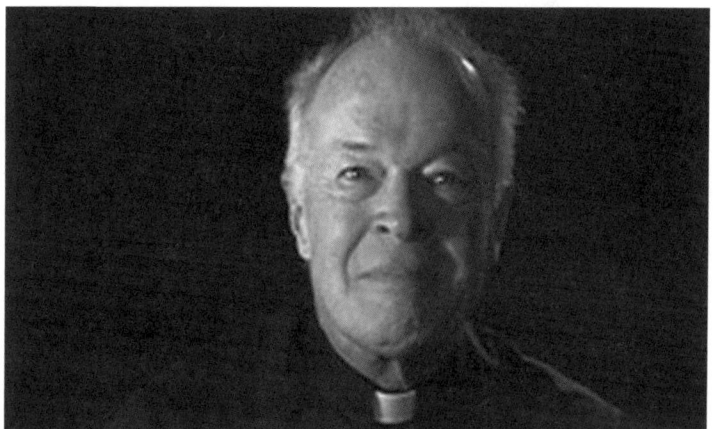

After 41 years of being a Catholic priest, I know people with tons of wealth who are absolutely free and I know other people with lots of wealth who think about it, worry about it, talk about it constantly. I know people who have nothing and they are absolutely free and filled with life and love. So it isn't a question of what you have or don't have. It's what has you? It's what you do with it and how you use it. It's your own personal declaration of freedom. I'm free.

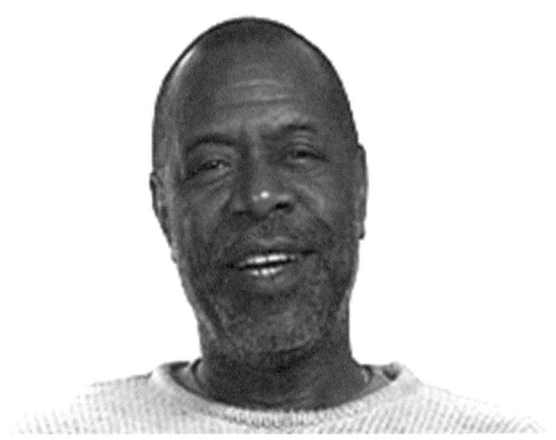

If I can love myself, I can love all, the world, the universe and everything in it. If I can generate that love, if I can touch someone each day and let them know that I love them no matter how they come to me, if I can show that I love, maybe that person will go away feeling a little better about themselves. But I have to have it inside me before I can give it to others. The love is what we need, pass it on. And that's touching souls.

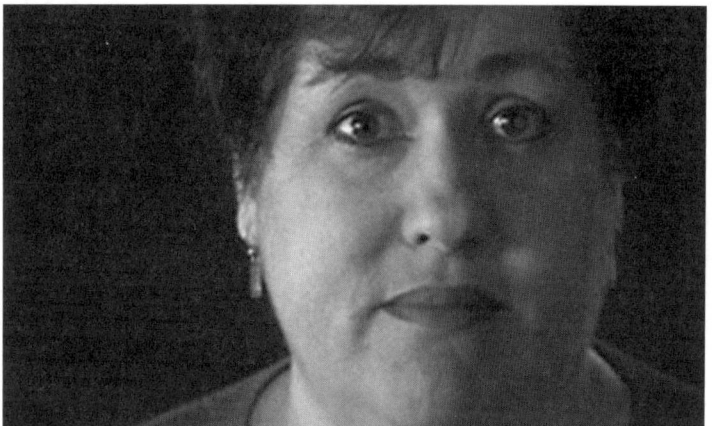

Humans can accomplish miraculous things, and we are really spectacular organisms and there's a limit and we will die, and the thing we didn't ask for will occur. So to live in the joy and the ecstasy, and the thrill of being loved and loving, and at the same time fully understanding that we are vulnerable and that we are fragile. To do the dance between the both of those is for me finding what really living this life is about. To live happily, joyfully and purposefully and fiercely when you are feeling vulnerable and afraid and fragile all at the same time, is the gift of life.

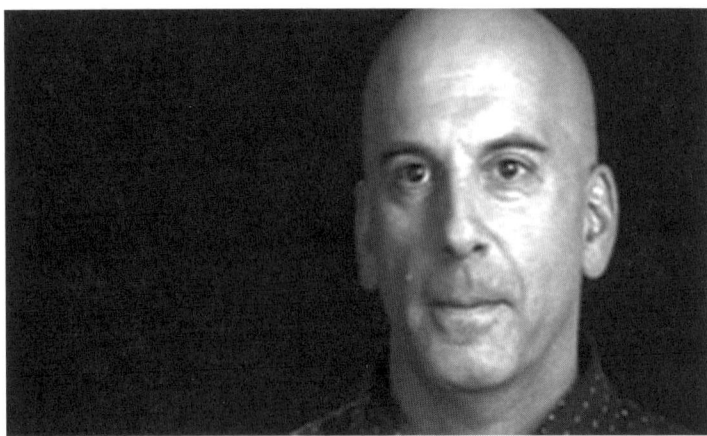

I believe that you have to base your happiness on your heart, treasures of your heart. There are experiences in life, people we love are the real valuable things. Everything else is really impermanent. It's hard in this materialistic environment we live in and everything is based on what we have physically. People tend to base their happiness on those things and that is when trouble begins. To base our happiness on the heart and how our inter-connectiveness is with other people is really where true happiness can come from.

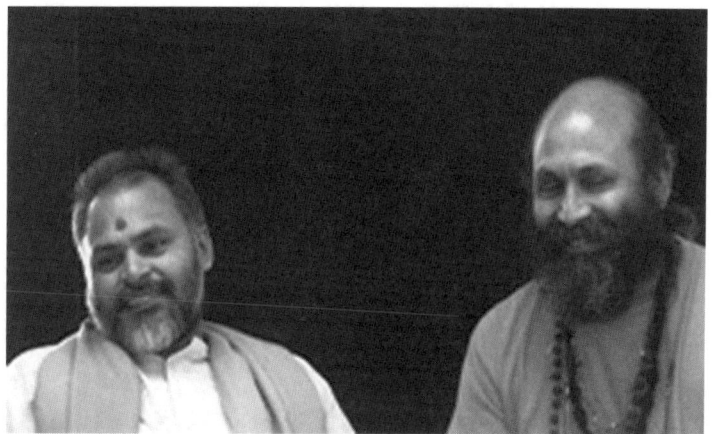

No matter what you are doing, what work you are doing, the most important thing is what is your attitude towards what you are doing. So whatever you do, offer that to the universe so that becomes the universe. Religion is not a separate subject. Whatever action you take towards your life and the society you live in, the most important thing is that you do it with a sense of sacrificial purpose for the universe.

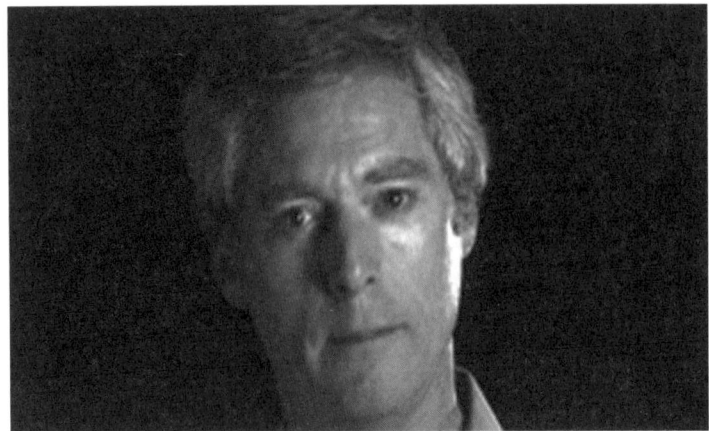

The awareness of impermanence, of the transient nature of human relationships, can actually open the heart more deeply to empathy, to love,
kindness, compassion, as one values the very presence of the other person
for the sake of that other person and not just I value this person because of
what this person can do for me. It shifts priorities. Because the awareness
of impermanence, of my own death is never very far away. To be able to
maintain very healthy awareness of one's mortality is a powerful ingredient
for living authentically.

PRESENCE

I'm here only for a small insignificant time, but that does not lessen the importance of this presence.

PERSPECTIVE and PRESENCE
David LaRocca, Ph.D.

"The *edifice of your pride* has to be dismantled. And that is terribly hard work." -Ludwig Wittgenstein

"How can we contrive to be at once astonished at the world and yet at home in it?" -G. K. Chesterton

Whenever I ascend into a fury of pride, fall into a bout of narcissism, or indulge the righteous delight of being overly serious about things, I contemplate the distance to the nearest star, or recall walks taken in the Niagara Gorge, 500 million years below the surface of Main Street. The sheer difficulty of such thinking—and its implications for the importance of my life—is humbling. What does it mean for light to travel at 186,000 miles per second, and for such rapidly moving energy to take six years to reach the nearest star? How does one conceive of a process of sedimentation that could result in but a thin layer of rock every few million years? If it is hard to understand these scales and durations, how difficult is it to comprehend that a life of about thirty thousand days isn't really that long or important or permanent after all? Trying to fathom the extreme, almost incomprehensible diminuitiveness and brevity of my human life brings me back to earth, as it were, reminding me of what is right in front of me, and that I am here experiencing it. Part of that new awareness may generate a feeling of awful estrangement, and imply a radical human insignificance. Being humbled by this overwhelming insight, however, is a decoy for what we are really after in trying to assess our sense of place.

In order to develop a new condition for thinking, in which I can be truly receptive to what is deeply consoling and helpfully reorienting about geological and astronomical time scales, I must not feel humiliated. Besides, one's conviction that he is but a speck of floating dust is really just pride working in reverse. I have replaced my false importance with false humility. Proud of my humility, I am comforted only by the sham reassurance that I have achieved some perspective because I am small and alone. Engaging the brutal fact of the expanding universe, baffling in scope, is genuinely comforting only when we feel our essential attendance in the order of things, not the fact of our insignificance. When we find ourselves in the universe, lost in it but also part of it, then we can recognize what is otherwise obscured by the millions of miles and billions of years: that I am not only in the present, but am always only there.

When philosophers and theologians refer to eternity, it seems they must be soliciting the idea of the atemporal. Eternity would feel like everything all at once because there is nowhere else for it to be. And yet, for humans what else is that superabundant wholeness, that tangible plentitude, but the present, the space we're always in, and can't get beyond? In this way, the present is eternal. Here. Now. And despite human memory that conjures the past, and human imagination that envisions the future, we remain forever where we are: in an unbounded moment called the present. Becoming more aware of the present, we begin to comprehend the only possible home for human thinking. Past and future are moods we undergo, or aspects we recognize. Yet, the present has the potential to be a state of genuine habitation. One can "live in the past or future" as easily as one can live on Alpha Centauri, but immanent life is only found in the unrestrained breadth of ever-immediate presence. Wherever we are, we can find ourselves. In order to accommodate the impressions of memory (the past) and the prospects created in imagination (the future), we need a direct, instantaneous, and atemporal present. The present is the workshop of experience, the state of affairs in which we draw together what has happened with what we think or want or believe will happen.

The potential benefit of an inhabited present is the sensation of feeling at home in the world. But how can one speak of being at home in the world one inhabits? We hear a late-breaking news announcement that a gas cloud is set to collide with the Milky Way, become reasonably alarmed by what sounds like a warning of impending destruction, and ask urgently—When? Awaiting a reply in the story, we learn that contact isn't expected for another 20 million years. Okay, so, not really of imminent concern. Yet, there is reason for some distress. What of this galaxy, of this world, of human life, of my life, could possibly matter then? Looking back-ward, the age of the universe is currently estimated to be 13,700 million years old (with a margin of error plus or minus 200 million years). The margin of error is about fifty times as long as the age of the oldest hominid fossil (somewhere around 3.6 million years), and about a thousand times as long as current estimates have the first homo sapiens walking around in Africa (about 200,000 years ago). What could possibly matter in this time scale and scheme of distances? How does one come to feel at home in a world that is so vast, so transient—and yet seemingly so profoundly more substantial than ourselves? And what do we really mean by "world" anyway? The literal earth is about 4.5 billion years old. Astrological and geological time are beyond any human scale or mode of comprehension; our analogies give us pictures and scenarios to contemplate, but no realities. Our notion of world or worlds may take flight from the duration of a planet's existence, or the distance between stars; but it is from our sense of alienation from those other-worldly facts that we are given a perspective on our own inhabitation in the present. We can see where we stand right now. Being at home, then, must be a matter of being present to the world.

What helps me be present—or feel at home in the world—is not will. I cannot exert a certain kind of mental effort to gain perspec-tive. Rather, in meditating on vast distances and mesmerizing time-scales, I may become more receptive to the present as a state of affairs that exceeds my will. In that way, in that spirit, I am truly humbled, which is to say, truly present.

Feeling at home feels like being where one is. Still, that feeling rarely manifests itself as safety, comfort, peace, or even a blasé calm in the familiar—for being present to the world often is fraught with anxiety, displacement, lostness, confusion, and turmoil. Be-ing present rarely puts us at ease. Yet, when we are no longer tempted to celebrate our insignificance, and no longer convinced that insight is a matter of willfulness, thoughts of vast, seemingly endless space, and incomprehensible scales of time will not demoralize or create despair. Rather, they reveal the unique possibilities for being at home in the world. Such present-minded attention does not mean one knows where one is, but that one is. And the sheer fact of that realization—that one is here at this moment—can transform consciousness into an expansive, ongoing experience of one's immediacy. The ever-present present, the "home" one inhabits from first breath to last, must be this supremely human dwelling.

BIBLIOGRAPHY

Richard Harris, "Gas Cloud Headed for Milky Way Collision" January 11, 2008.
http://www.npr.org/templates/story/story.php?storyId=18027001

Ludwig Wittgenstein. Culture and Value. G. H. von Wright, ed. Chicago: The University of Chicago Press, 1980, p. 26e.

G. K. Chesterton. Orthodoxy. Stilwell, Kansas: Digireads, 2005, p. 7.

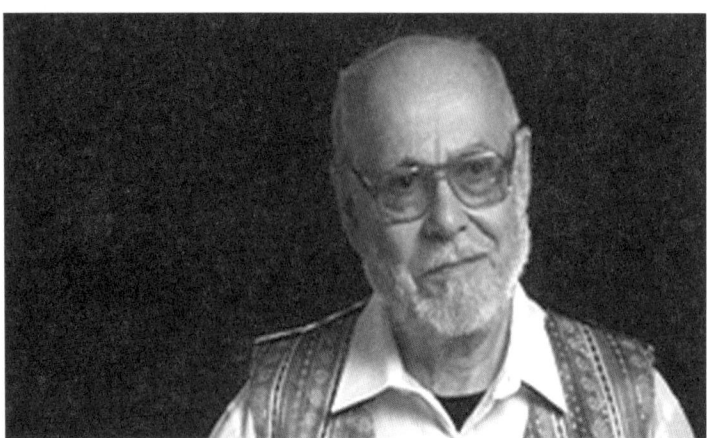

Presence, what do I do with it? We come to life involuntarily. We did not have a choice. And we leave involuntarily. We don't have a choice.

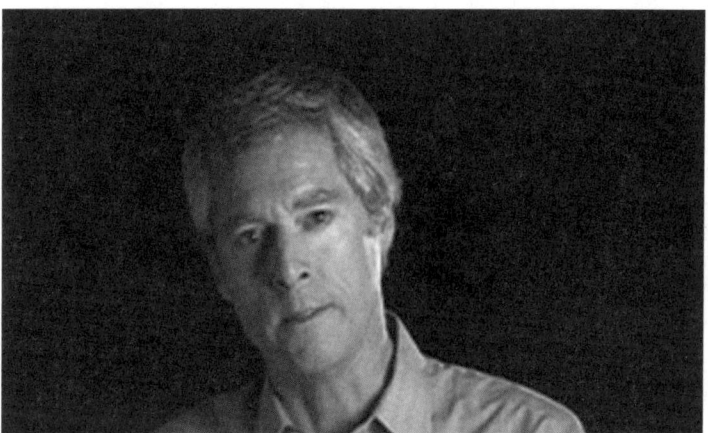

This reality of impermanence, this awareness of impermanence winds up being like a torch. It comes in and burns off the chaff, burns off the debris and leaves only that which is truly of value.

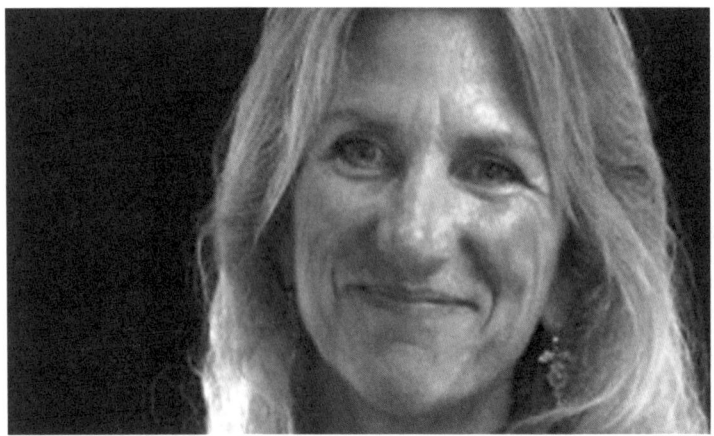

This day is precious, this life is precious and I have a greater commitment to coming up with some resolution now rather than thinking later is going to be here. Impermanence is real, it's the nature of life and to be aware of that, and find a way to stay aware of that daily, can really help give us a feeling of gratitude that makes every day better, every interaction better and makes it possible to create a peaceful world. Everything becomes so precious because it's so temporary and transient.

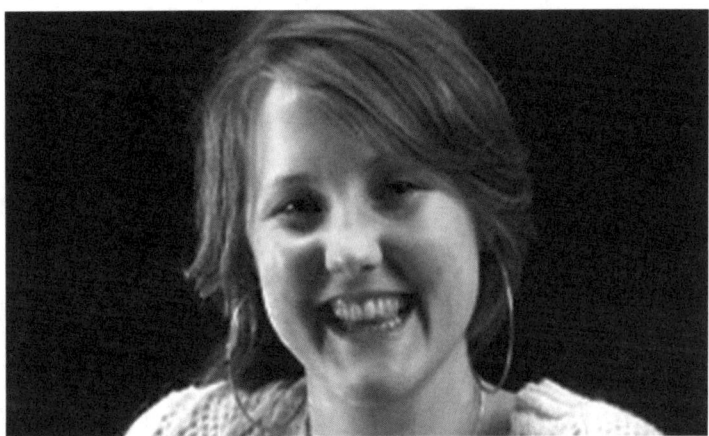

If the golden years were now instead of later, then people would live a more peaceful life and just do the things they always talk about wanting to do later now.

The most frightening experience for me was getting what I want. It's no longer in the future. Now I have it and now I have to do something with it. Being aware of impermanence can sometimes fire you up to get everything done before it's over. Do I hold off or jump in and go for it? I'm going to be here just for the day, let's live it up. Who knows what's coming tomorrow?

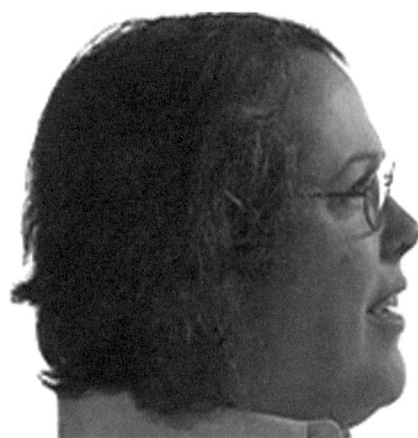

When you think you are immortal when you are younger, there's certain desire and certain striving to get somewhere so it feels very self-important. There's a lot of ego in it. It's about you and what you can accomplish, what your life is about and how you'll make meaning of it. With that comes a lot of stress, worrying about failure, how it looks like, judged by other people.

Now at this point of my life, I really embrace impermanence and welcome it. It's a way to be present and be here now in the moment. It's a way to take ego out a little bit of your day-to-day life. It's easier to do the things I care about, that I find meaning from and I work just as hard but I'm not attached to them the same way so it makes the whole living experience that much more real and enjoyable.

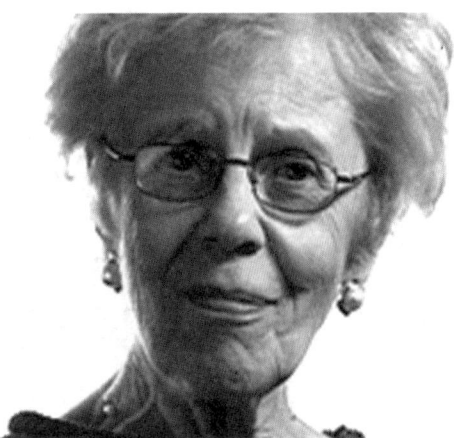

You have to appreciate each day for what it has to offer. A nice part of growing old is to have pleasant memories. They are important to me. I don't think I could have survived without having had good memories to recall. It just makes life worth living.

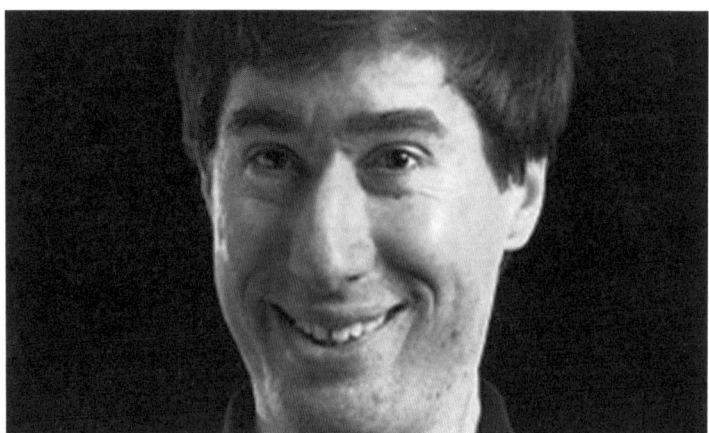

You have to make a conscious effort in whatever you are going to do in your life. The choices you will make for this day for your lifetime even if it's going to be another ten years or forty years, it's still limited. If you are less attached to these things that are fleeting, you can let go of a lot of stress. There's no focus of the mind like the prisoner who has a fortnight to live. He knows what he is going to do, what he's going to be thinking about for that short period of time.

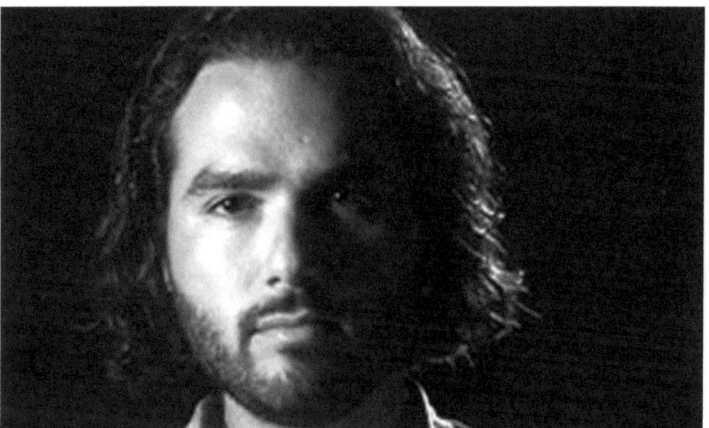

Coming to terms with the nature of time, the nature of something that is past and no longer retrievable and the future that is ahead of us and always forever unreachable demands some kind of attention to the present. The present is impermanent, the present is a space of constant change, it's the space of heartbeat, space of brain pulses and blood flowing and rays coming from the sun and waves crashing, it's the space of temperature and circulation. To be present is to live in impermanence.

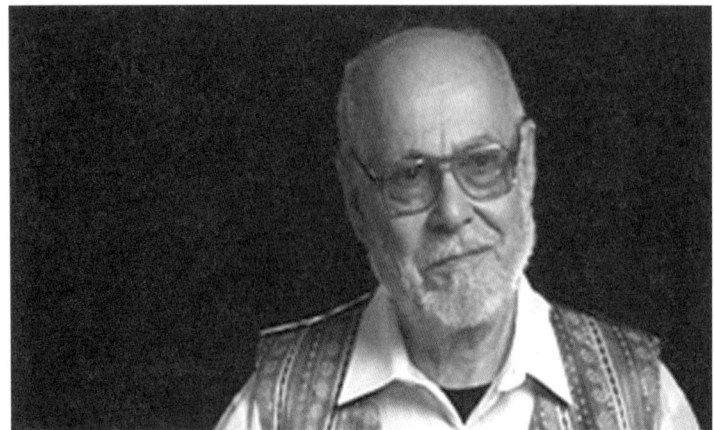

The realization of my presence as a speck on this earth and the earth being a speck in the larger universe has added a great deal of meaning to my life. Every moment became precious. My life, day-to-day, became very significant to create and to live it to its potential. I'm here only for a small insignificant time, but that does not lessen the importance of this presence.

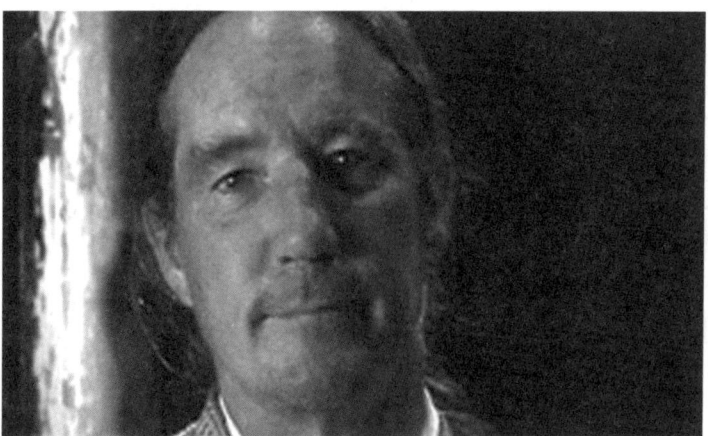

The idea that you can't really hold on to anything, that it is all impermanent and you are blessed with presence and that presence is made up of
memories, your tactile experience in the moment and your expectation of
the future, I believe we as humans are built out of very tactile memory that
insists we engage. Engaging requires memory and expectation or antici-
pation without either of which the moment loses meaning. It's much more
easily said than done.

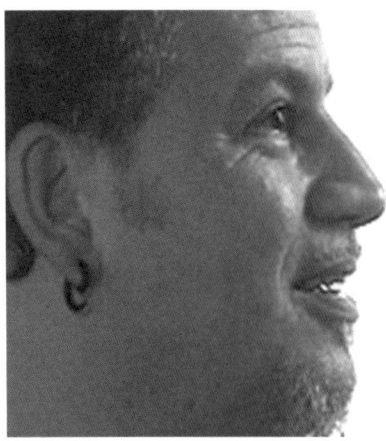

I'm in traffic, I'm trying to get somewhere so I'm definitely in my permanent old school attention frame of mind and there's a bumper sticker that says, "Live like you are dying," like you are passing, like you are impermanent, and actually wakes you up to everything you need right now. More than you can possibly have imagined before. It's born into that moment. It's like an impulse, the catalyst for awareness that would wake the dead.

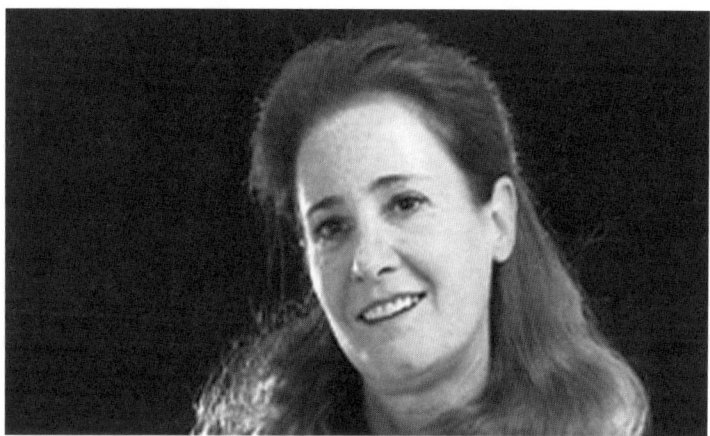

I never thought of life in terms of time parameters at all. When I hear people say, "life is short," I roll my eyes. For me, life is long when you compare to any other species with a few exceptions. It's a long time. I don't think that a number is any measure of whether your life is long or short. So when people die in their eighties, people say "oh they had a good long life" and I think just because it was long doesn't mean that it was anything but long.

Presence

A few around a table
In a corner on the planet
Binding the whole universe
At a moment in time,
A wink of time
That lasts forever.
Presence
Enduring for time immeasurably
While passing from one phase to another,
Is continuous presence.

Elias Abu-Saba
11/07/2004
Half Moon Bay

Presence Without Matter

Voices are heard
Without a ripple
Of a sound
Floating around.

Thoughts are read
Without a word
Or a sign
Of any design.

Love is shared
Without the fear
That the lover
One day will disappear.

A lovely rose
Never asked,
Filled the air
With fragrance.

You spoke and I heard
Not in words or in signs,
For you and I were born as one
Not in space or in time,
Sailing across the universe
Where the wings have failed.
Your voice alone
Drew the compass and steered my ship
Rocking fearlessly in the unknown.

Elias Abu-Saba, from *Songs in Time*, 1973

Essayists

Tenzin Tethong is president of The Dalai Lama Foundation and distinguished fellow of the Tibetan Studies Initiative at Stanford University. He is a former representative of His Holiness the Dalai Lama, and a driving force behind the establishment of key Tibetan initiatives such as the Tibetan Youth Congress and the International Campaign for Tibet, and the recently established Center for Altruism and Compassion Research and Education at the Medical School of Stanford University.

B. Alan Wallace began his studies of Tibetan Buddhism, language, and culture in 1970 at the University of Göttingen in Germany and then continued his studies over the next fourteen years in India, Switzerland, and the United States. Ordained as a Buddhist monk by H. H. the Dalai Lama in 1975, he has taught Buddhist meditation and philosophy worldwide since 1976 and has served as interpreter for numerous Tibetan scholars and contemplatives, including the Dalai Lama. Having earned his undergraduate degree at Amherst College, he returned his monastic vows and went on to earn his Ph.D. in religious studies at Stanford University. He is the founder and president of the Santa Barbara Institute for Consciousness Studies.

Kay Larson is an art critic (*New York Magazine* 1980-94; *the New York Times* and other independent critical writing 1994-present); editor (currently, managing editor, curator: *The Museum Journal*); and educator (currently, writing tutor, Center for Curatorial Studies, Bard College, Annandale on Hudson, New York). She is working on a book entitled *Where the Heart Beats: John Cage, Zen Buddhism, and the Inner Life of Artists*. Since 1972, her articles and criticism have appeared in a range of publications: museum catalogues, art magazines, newspapers, and the popular press. She began Buddhist practice at Zen Mountain Monastery in Mt. Tremper, New York, and is now a practitioner of Tibetan Buddhism in the Karma Kagyu lineage, based at Karma Triyana Dharmachakra, Woodstock, New York.

Lucy Hilmer is a San Francisco photographer, poet, and documentary filmmaker obsessed with the passage of time. Her autobiographical black and white photographs form ongoing series-in-time, and are the subjects of three books and one film currently in production. *Birthday Suits* are self-portraits (1974–present) made each year on her birthday in her white lollypop underpants, shoes and socks. *The Wedding House* images (1985–present) are self-portraits made with her husband on their anniversaries. And *My Valentines* (1987–2009) are photographic postcards showing their daughter growing up in relationship to a rose and her father's hand. Each series constitutes a book, and also flows into a film, *Stopping Time*, about a photographer trying to stop time with images. Hilmer's poetry provides narrative for her books and soundtrack for her film.

Growing up in India, **Kavita N. Ramdas** learned firsthand about discrimination. Her commitment to justice and gender equality was strengthened by an activist mother, Mount Holyoke College, and graduate studies in development. After working with non-profits in India, Kavita was program officer for community development and population at the John D. and Catherine T. MacArthur Foundation in Chicago. She leads the Global Fund for Women, the world's largest grant-making foundation exclusively funding international women's rights groups. During her tenure, assets have tripled, enabling the fund to award $8.5 million annually to organizations in 167 countries. Recently appointed an advisor on global development to the Bill and Melinda Gates Foundation, she is also a prolific writer and public speaker on human rights and international development.

Philip A. Pizzo, M.D., has been dean of the Stanford School of Medicine since April 2001. Before joining Stanford, he was the physician-in-chief of Children's Hospital in Boston and chair of the Department of Pediatrics at Harvard Medical School from 1996-2001. Between 1973 and 1996 Pizzo served as head of the National Cancer Institute's infectious disease section, chief of the NCI's pediatric branch, and acting scientific director for NCI's Division of Clinical Sciences. Pizzo devoted much of his career to the diagnosis, management, prevention and treatment of childhood cancers and the infectious complications that occur in children and adults whose immune systems are compromised by cancer and AIDS. He and his research team pioneered the development of new treatments for children with HIV infection as well as numerous other innovations in cancer and infectious diseases more broadly. He is the author of more than 500 scientific articles and 14 books. He has received numerous awards and honors and is a member of a number of prestigious organizations and societies.

David LaRocca writes on philosophy, religion, rhetoric, and film, and works on photography and film projects. Author of *On Emerson* (Wadsworth 2002) and editor of Stanley Cavell's *Emerson's Transcendental Etudes* (Stanford 2003), his essays are published in anthologies and scholarly journals such as *Film and Philosophy, Epoché, Transactions,* and *The Review of Metaphysics*. He studied at SUNY-Buffalo, Berkeley, Vanderbilt, and Harvard, and is presently consulting producer and editor of the documentary film series *Intellectual Portraits*. He lives in New York City.

Biographies

Mihai Nadin's career combines science, art, technology, and the humanities. He is often described as a Renaissance personality. Nadin holds advanced degrees in electrical engineering and computer science and a post-doctoral degree in philosophy, logic and the theory of science. Nadin believes in applying knowledge for future contexts rather than glorifying past achievements for their own sake. Through his research, spanning from engineering to mathematics, digital technology, philosophy, semiotics, theory of mind, and, most recently, anticipatory systems, he asserts an integrated understanding of the world. His publications include hundreds of articles and over 20 books; he has also authored novels, poems, and plays. In 2004, Nadin accepted an endowed chair at The University of Texas at Dallas, where he heads the antÉ Institute for Research in Anticipatory Systems.

Anne Firth Murray, a New Zealander, is the founding president of the Global Fund for Women. She is a consulting professor in human biology at Stanford University. Ms. Murray serves on the boards of several non-profit organizations, including the Global Justice Center, Grass Roots Alliance for Community Education, and UNNITI, a fund in India. She has received awards and honors for her work on women's health and philanthropy, and in 2005 she was nominated as one of 1,000 women for the Nobel Peace Prize. Her book *Paradigm Found: Leading and Managing for Positive Change* was published in May, 2006. Her most recent book, *From Outrage to Courage: Women Taking Action for Health and Justice*, was published in December 2007.

Elias Georges Abu-Saba was born in 1929 in Sidon, Lebanon, where he graduated from the American University of Beirut (BS), and then from Virginia Polytechnic Institute and State University (M.A. and Ph.D.). He won the Clarency Shedd Fellowship to study at the Pacific School of Religion in Berkeley pursuing his passion for contemplation, ethics, poetry, and politics. Elias was always both poet and engineer, translating his visions into words and soaring structures. He taught in the engineering schools of Bucknell University and Bradley University, and retired as full professor from North Carolina A&T State University. He died in 2006 and is survived by his wife Mary Bentley Abu-Saba, two children, Leila and Khalil, and three grandchildren. His first book of poetry *Songs in Time* was published in 1973.

Artists

Video artists **David Hodge** and **Hi-Jin Kang Hodge** come from an internationally recognized background in industrial and graphic design. After years of designing products and corporate communications for clients such as Apple, Sony, Herman Miller, and NTT DoCoMo, they now create documentaries and artistic installations that explore a diverse range of topics. Their works, which have been shown in exhibitions around the world, typically blend editorial materials with innovative uses of technology. Thematically, they seek to identify foundational principles in the human condition and expand on them through multiple viewpoints. David and Hi-Jin's work encompasses many new and traditional types of media. They've shown ocean views on the side of a 40-story office building in downtown Seoul and were the first to use video iPods in an artistic installation. Today, they continue to evolve as artists, always looking for new ways to bring video and other media to bear on pressing social questions.

Interviewees

Dianne Derby	Annika Lindquist	Kayoko Fujita
Clifford Hunt	Jens Persson	Abbas Zaidi
Miles O'Riley	Sheri Kramer	Goerge McCann
Mihai Nadin	Art Melar	Lisa Shiveley
Mauro Di Nucci	James Labinski	Andrew Clayton
Judy-Johnson WIlliams	Pelerouge	Laura Rubio
Viviana Guzman	Mary Magocsy	Jeff Smith
Davd Larocca	Lisa Petrides	Melissa Lane
Michael Olivola	Rob Carpenter	Jim Lane
Harold Fethe	Jeremy Basserman	Joe Okies
Ray Day	Isabella Betkowski	Greg Lynn
Dick Charnock	Carrie Hollister	Thomas Dolby
Dale Charnock	Kim Evans	Harper Robertson
Peter Summersgil	Jessica Heidt	Ellen Rose
Alan Wallace	Oliver Warner	Marge Trogden
Elias Abu-Suba	Lou Baily Boyle	Eric Schou
Tenzin Tethong	Logan Kahle	Ken Rowe
Taylor McCormick	Caslon Kahle	Alan Baral
Rick Knoblaugh	Zachary Donnenfield	Keaton Shiveley
Neil Rolnick	Mary Austin	Vicki Malherek-McCoy
Monina Dolan	Brewster Kahle	Therese Schou
Gray Holland	Ann Hodge	Corrine Morita
Young soo Lee	Lisa Mulhardt	George Arriola
Mark Morris Goodman	Brian Jones	Elise Hunt
Mavis Muller	Elizabeth Nadin	Alex Subrizi
Michael Dolan	Carl Tape	Steve Hawk
Chris Ridgeway	Hee jung Yoon	David Stark
Firehawk	Rayn Carnrick	Darlene Markovich
Lucy Hilmer	Tekla Subrizi	Steve Markovich
Gisela Schecter	Janet Kern	Peg Atkinson
Todd Gilbert	Melinda Thompson	Mary Delong
Ringit Gürlich	Susanne Eliott	Kimberly Carter
Bunthoe Un Hack	David Buyer	Foster Gamble
Estria Miyashiro	Katja Wessling Subrizi	Pam Higgins
Stephanie Krassner	Swami Sharnanandsi maharaj	Dario Campanile
Bill Veltrop	Param Sadhvi Matasaraswati maharaj	Tsering Vassallo
Gretchen McCoy	Rukmami Sujan	Gionvanni Vassallo
Jennnifer Huang	Laurence Freeman	Arjia Rinpoche
Joy Kutaka-kennedy	Nori Tolson	Lynn Mosier
Mark Moulton	Terry Green	Drake Mosier
Tony Hoberg	Ken French	

Acknowledgments

With a project as extensive as this one, we have many people to thank. Darlene Markovich, Ron Haak, and the Committee of 100 for Tibet conceived, organized, and implemented The Missing Peace: Artists Consider the Dalai Lama exhibition, and for that we are very grateful. We'd also like to thank Tenzin Tethong for his invaluable help in the entire Impermanence project, and particularly with this book. In addition we would like to thank the good people at Snow Lion Publications, Sidney Piburn, Jeffrey M. Cox, and Liz Green for their direction, guidance, and for seeing this book to completion.

There are a number of people who offered their artistic, technical, and intellectual talents during the Impermanence project. Harold Fethe provided valuable ideas early in the project, Michael Lazar authored the DVD, and Joe Shepter made a substantial contribution as a ghostwriter. The bands Crystal Spirits and Sisters of the Sound Continuum contributed music to the project.(*)
We'd especially like to thank James Labinski for his tireless efforts in creating the soundtrack for the installation and the DVD.

We'd like to thank our contributing essayists B. Alan Wallace, Kay Larson, Lucy Hilmer, Kavita Ramdas, Philip A. Pizzo, MD, Mihai Nadin, Anne Firth Murray, David LaRocca, and Elias and Mary Abu-Saba for their insight and their time.

Needless to say, the 125 people who sat in front of our cameras were also integral to the success of this project. Without their wisdom and openness, Impermanence would not have been the revelation it was. Their names are listed on page 156.

We are grateful for the support of BBI Engineering, Digital Pond, Kino Flow, Lunar Design, New Wave Entertainment, Proteus Design, Silicon Image, Timex Corporation, Garthwait & Griffin Films, Peg Atkinson, Dan Butler, Craig Clarke, Clifford & Leslie Hunt, Janet Kern, Jim & Melissa Lane, Greg Lynn, Gretchen McCoy & Vicki Malherek-McCoy, Ed & Sumya Miner, Lynne Mosier, Vicki Olds, Darrel Rhea, Howie & Susan Rosen, Michael & Casimiera Shapiro, Alex & Katja Subrizi.

In addition, we'd like to recognize Randy Rosenberg, curator of the Missing Peach exhibition. We would like to thank our hosts at the museums where the exhibition appeared, including Marla Berns at the Fowler Museum of Cultural History in Los Angeles; Pam Ambrose at the Loyola University Museum of Art in Chicago; Tim Henry at Rubin Museum of Art in New York; Ken Foster, Renee De Guzman, and Kate Eilertsen at Yerba Buena Center for the Arts in San Francisco; Jessica Lonegren, Frank Lonegren, Michelle Townsend, and Jane Munro at SPUR Projects; and Seiichi Mizuno and Ms. Kuichi Midori and Hillside Terrace in Tokyo.

Finally, we'd like to recognize the work and sacrifice of His Holiness the Dalai Lama and the Tibetan people, whose patient struggle has been an inspiration to us at every stage of the project.

(*) Crystal Spirits: Micheline Bogey, Magali Noth, Daisy Ducret
  Sisters of the Sound Continuum: Nancy Beckman, Norma Codova, Una Nakamura, Suzanne Parkhurst, Kellen Perry, Maryliz Smith, Karolyn van Putten, Mary Watkins

The following instructions have been provided to help you to explore this unique DVD.

Impermanence is presented as a 75 minute multi-part program that re-creates the experience of the original installation. Once started, the main Impermanence program plays in an endless loop. Playback may be interrupted by pressing the "menu" or "title" key on your remote control. This takes you to the main menu where you can access additional features of this DVD.

During playback you will view a number of "interview mosaics" over which a button icon will appear. That button icon looks something like this:

If you press the "enter" key on your remote control at these points, playback will switch to a new program that plays all of the individual interviews in the mosaic, one after another. It takes about 6 - 8 minutes to watch all the interviews.

In this mode, a navigational element at the bottom of the screen lets you know where you are in the set. That navigational element looks something like this:

01 02 03 04 05 **06** 07 08 09 10 11 12 13 14 15 16 ▲

The upward pointing triangle on the far right is a button that allows you to return to the main Impermanence program loop. Just press the "enter" (or "menu") key on your remote. You will be returned at a point just after the end of the interview mosaic you interrupted. If you watch all of the interviews in the set you will be returned to the main Impermanence program loop at this same point.

Thanks for reading. Enjoy the disc!

Contents of DVD

Impermanence
a 25-minute version of the original installation which plays in a continuous loop.

Impermanence Highlights
twelve additional segments of individual responses to the Impermanence questions. (*)

An interview with B. Allan Wallace

An interview with Laurence Freeman

Realizing Impermanence
a time-lapse video showing the installation setup @ YBCA.

The Music of Impermanence
video excerpts from the recording sessions with Crystal Spirits and The Sisters of the Sound Continuum.

(*) Accessed as a special feature during playback of the main Impermanence program. See the instructions for the DVD on how to view the highlights on page 158.